THE COMPLETE GUIDE TO MULTIMATE

THE COMPLETE GUIDE TO MULTIMATE™

Carol Holcomb Dreger

San Francisco • Paris • Düsseldorf • London

Cover art by Judithe Sager

DIF is a trademark of Microsoft Corporation.
IBM is a registered trademark and IBM PC is a trademark of International Business Machines.
Linguibase is a trademark of Proximity Devices Corporation.
MultiMate is a trademark of MultiMate International Corporation.
SYBEX is a registered trademark of SYBEX, Inc.

SYBEX is not affiliated with any manufacturer.

Every effort has been made to supply complete and accurate information. However, SYBEX assumes no responsibility for its use, nor for any infringements of patents or other rights of third parties which would result.

Copyright©1984 SYBEX Inc., 2021 Challenger Drive #100, Alameda, CA 94501. World rights reserved. No part of this publication may be stored in a retrieval system, transmitted, or reproduced in any way, including but not limited to photocopy, photograph, magnetic or other record, without the prior agreement and written permission of the publisher.

Library of Congress Card Number: 84-51795
ISBN 0-89588-229-9
Manufactured in the United States of America
20 19 18 17 16 15 14 13 12 11

To Donn, who (even though he now will *never* send me flowers) deserves at least a book dedication for his support and patience this past year.

ACKNOWLEDGMENTS

Although nearly everyone with whom an author in mid-project comes in contact becomes involved, the following deserve special mention for their part in *The Complete Guide to MultiMate*: Roger Franklin of Syntax Systems who started it all by introducing me to MultiMate and selling me a computer; Dorothy Beutow, Campus Bookstore Manager, for her advice on publishers and enthusiasm for my idea; Barbara Patterson, who with *The Successful Woman* helped prove it was possible to survive the birth of a book; Susan Simons and Mary Peters, who used early versions of the manuscript in their classes; their students (and mine), for providing valuable feedback; Karen and Fred Watterson of Shoreline Commuity College, who shared their technical expertise and enthusiasm for computers; Doug Henry, patient friend and fountain of computer knowledge; Gloria Campbell, who accepted the project of indexing; the many former and present Edmonds Community College computer lab personnel who have been so helpful, especially Wes Sims, Don Ullom, Dan Volkmann, Jeff Muzz, and Lee Fisher; and Becky Montgomery, who (as Edmonds Community College Math/Science Division Director) promotes an atmosphere that encourages and supports all who are interested in increasing their utilization of computers.

Finally, to Sally Waller and Leanna Holcomb (two especially good listeners) and to the rest of my dear friends and family—thank you for being so supportive and for tolerating my preoccupation this past year.

Carol Holcomb Dreger
October, 1984

CONTENTS

INTRODUCTION xix

1 A FEW PRELIMINARIES 2

The Keyboard 2
Inserting Disks into Drives 6
Loading DOS and MultiMate 6
The Main Menu 8
On-Screen Prompts 9
The Help Facility 10
Summary of Operations Covered in this Chapter 12

2 CREATING A NEW DOCUMENT 15

The Create a New Document Screen 15
The Document Summary Screen 17
The Modify Document Defaults Screen 19
The Status Line 21
The Format Line 21
Word Wrap 22
Exiting the Document 24
Removing the Disks From the Disk Drives 25
An Opportunity to Practice 25
Summary of Operations Covered in this Chapter 27

3 MOVING THE CURSOR 29

Moving to the Next Word 29
Moving to the First or Last Character in a Line 30
Screen Capacity 30
Getting to the First or Last Character on a Screen or Page 32
Making Bigger Jumps 32
Summary of Operations Covered in this Chapter 33

4 EDITING A DOCUMENT 35

Strikeover 35
Inserting a Single Character 36

Deleting a Single Character   37

Inserting More Than One Character   38

Correcting While in Insert Mode   39

Deleting More Than One Character   40

Highlighting Methods   41

Dehighlighting Methods   43

A Combination of Methods   44

Saving a Document   45

Recalling a Document   46

Summary of Operations Covered in this Chapter   46

5 FORMATTING A DOCUMENT 49

A Comparison of Typewriter Formatting
  with MultiMate Formatting   49

Thinking in Terms of Spaces in the Writing Line   49

The Limits of the Screen Display   50

General Information about Format Lines   50

The System Default Format Line   51

Inserting Format Lines within a Document   51

Modifying a Format Line   52

Creating an Alternate Format Line
  within a Document   54

Deleting a Format Line   55

Summary of Operations Covered in this Chapter   56

6 ADVANCED FORMATTING FUNCTIONS: PAGINATION   59

Automatic Page Breaks   59
Changing the Number of Lines Per Page   59
Manually Creating New Pages   60
Deleting Page Breaks to Combine Pages   61
Automatically Repaginating a Document   61
Required Page Breaks   62
Deleting Required Page Breaks   63
Moving Through Pages   63
Using the Place Mark Function   64
Summary of Operations Covered in this Chapter   64

7 SPECIAL FEATURES   69

Center   69
Indent   70
Decimal Tabs   72
Hardspaces (Required Spaces)   73
Soft Hyphens and Hard Hyphens   74
Auto Underline-Text and Deunderline   76
Auto Underline-Alphanumeric   77
Superscript and Subscript   77
Ending this Session   78
Summary of Operations Covered in this Chapter   78

8 PRINTING A DOCUMENT — 83

A Word About Terminology   83
Readying the Printer   83
Accessing the Printing Process   84
The Submit a Document for Printing Screen   84
Summary of Operations Covered in this Chapter   91

9 OTHER PRINT FUNCTIONS — 93

The Print Screen Key   93
Stopping Printing Temporarily   93
Stopping Printing Permanently   94
Special Print Modes   95
Changing Pitch within a Document   97
Accessing Printer Control Utilities   98
Summary of Operations Covered in this Chapter   101

10 ADVANCED EDITING FUNCTIONS THAT RELOCATE TEXT: MOVE, COPY, AND EXTERNAL COPY — 105

The Move Function   105
Uses of the Move Function   108

The Copy Function   108
Uses of the Copy Function   111
The External Copy Function   111
Uses of the External Copy Function   112
Summary of Operations Covered in this Chapter   112

11 ADVANCED EDITING FUNCTIONS: SEARCH AND REPLACE   117

The Importance of Spaces and Punctuation   117
The Search Function   117
The Replace Function   119
Deleting with Replace   120
Format Line Replace   121
Summary of Operations Covered in this Chapter   122

12 LIBRARY FUNCTIONS   125

Creating a Library Document   125
Attaching a Library Document   127
Recalling Library Entries   128
Possible Entries in a Standard Library Document   129
Summary of Operations Covered in this Chapter   130

13 MERGE FUNCTIONS 133

Creating the Primary Document 133
Creating the Secondary Document 134
Printing the Merged Documents 136
Troubleshooting When the Merge Function Doesn't Work 138
Printing Only One of Several Letters 139
An Unusual Situation to Watch Out For 139
Creating Envelopes from the Secondary Document 139
Summary of Operations Covered in this Chapter 140

14 AUTOMATIC HEADERS AND FOOTERS 143

Rules for Typing Page Numbers on Long Documents 143
Preparing Practice Documents 144
Creating up Automatic Headers 144
Special Print Instructions for Automatic Headers and Footers 145
Creating up Automatic Footers 146
Printing the Document Containing an Automatic Footer 147
Stopping a Header or Footer from Printing 148
Procedures for Setting up Alternating Headers or Footers 148
How to Type "Page X Out of Fifteen Pages" 149
Using Roman Numerals in Headers and Footers 149
Summary of Operations Covered in this Chapter 150

15 COLUMN MANIPULATION FUNCTIONS — 153

Column Insert 153
Column Delete 154
Column Move 155
Column Copy 156
Summary of Operations Covered in this Chapter 157

16 DOCUMENT HANDLING UTILITIES — 161

The Copy a Document Function 161
Uses of the Copy a Document Function 163
The Move a Document Function 163
Uses of the Move a Document Function 165
The Delete a Document Function 165
Uses of the Delete a Document Function 166
The Rename a Document Function 167
The Print Document Summary Screens Function 168
The Search Document Summary Screen Function 169
Summary of Operations Covered in this Chapter 171

17 KEY PROCEDURES — 175

Building a Key Procedure File 176

Executing a Key Procedure File 177
Editing a Key Procedure File 178
Summary of Operations Covered in this Chapter 179

18 USING THE SPELL CHECK AND SPELL EDIT FUNCTIONS 183

Capabilities of the Spell Check Function 183
After Spell Check—What Then? 183
How to Spell Check an Entire Document 184
How to Spell Check a Portion of a Document 186
Manually Correcting Errors Identified by Spell Check 186
Using Spell Edit to Correct Errors 187
A Final Word About Spell Check and Spell Edit 191
Summary of Operations Covered in this Chapter 191

APPENDICES

A OTHER UTILITIES 195

B MULTIMATE KEY COMBINATIONS FOR THE IBM PERSONAL COMPUTER 201

INDEX 205

INTRODUCTION

If you are a new user of the MultiMate word processing program, this book will help you get acquainted with your new tool by introducing you to all its features. *The Complete Guide to MultiMate* will explain functions, procedures, and terminology that you need to get the most from MultiMate. Even more important, it will suggest many practical ways to apply what you have learned to your everyday work situation.

If you have used the basic features of MultiMate for some time now and are now eager to move on to its more sophisticated aspects, you will find *The Complete Guide to MultiMate* useful as well. The first section of the book may serve as a review and reference for you. Reading descriptions of functions and processes may make something stick that didn't when you were first exposed to it, and you will find that the chapter summaries are helpful reviews.

If you are lucky enough to be quite experienced with MultiMate, the primary value of the book may be in learning special techniques which you have never learned before. As a lifelong student myself, I long ago discovered (to paraphrase Will Rogers): I never read a book from which I couldn't learn something. And, if you have figured out a special trick or timesaver that wasn't covered in this book, please write to me about it; I'll find a way to share it with as many MultiMate users as I can.

Finally, for those who aren't yet using MultiMate: most computer experts recommend that you choose software that does what you want and then pick the hardware that will run it. So, even if you are just thinking about purchasing word processing software, you will benefit from reading *The Complete Guide to MultiMate*. You will get a feel for what it will be like to use MultiMate because you are led through the functions and shown exactly what the screen displays will look like. You will also become familiar with word processing terminology, so when you hear a word processing program's features and functions described, you won't feel as though you are listening to a foreign language.

What MultiMate Can Do for You

If you are used to typing on a regular typewriter, throw away your correction fluid and chalk-backed paper and get ready for an exciting introduction into the efficiencies of word processing!

The MultiMate word processing program not only enhances your productivity, but allows you to concentrate on the more creative aspects of document preparation, such as content and formatting.

If you frequently have to compose letters or first drafts of reports, you'll appreciate how easy it is to revise using MultiMate. You can readily take that first step of getting something down because you know it's only a starting point and everything can be changed easily. You will type faster because the keyboard requires such a light touch, and you will type more accurately because you won't be so concerned about making errors—they are very easy to correct!

The text you type using MultiMate first appears on the display screen of your computer. It is committed to paper only after you issue a special printing instruction. You can see on the display screen exactly how your business letter or sales report will look before it is printed. If you don't like what you see, you can easily change it or even experiment with several different arrangements.

With MultiMate you will never again have to retype an entire balance sheet because of a couple of uncorrectable typing errors or because you want to change the margins or tab settings. When you do need to revise a page, what was correct remains correct; you need to change only the part that was not the way you wanted it. When margins and tabs are changed with MultiMate, the document immediately conforms to the new settings.

If you do much repetitive typing or use form letters or *boilerplate* paragraphs, you will find word processing especially useful. You can type something once and then recall and use it over and over. And with a special MultiMate feature called *background printing,* you can even work on one document while another is printing.

Using a word processor can also help you develop the very valuable skill of composing at the keyboard because it allows you to concentrate on getting your thoughts down as rapidly as you can. Your written communication skills will probably improve along with your word processing skills because rewriting is so easy. You can edit and revise your work until it represents the very best you have to offer.

For all of these reasons, you will soon be very glad you have this marvelous tool at your disposal.

Which Version of MultiMate Do You Have?

The Complete Guide to MultiMate is written to be used with MultiMate version 3.22. Versions of MultiMate prior to 3.20 won't have the Spelling Checker, the Key Procedures feature, or some of the enhancements to the printing function such as Shadow Print.

Although MultiMate has been successfully used on other computers, this book is written specifically for MultiMate as it operates on an IBM Personal Computer. The IBM PC described in this book has dual disk drives that use double-sided disks, has 256K bytes of memory, and uses the 1.1 version of DOS (Disk Operating System). The MultiMate users' manual describes other system configurations which will support the program as well.

How this Book Is Organized

The Complete Guide to MultiMate introduces MultiMate functions, explains how they work, and suggests potential uses. It also shows how the different features and functions of MultiMate can be used, often in combinations, for specific business applications. Throughout the book, examples are given for you to practice on, but you may choose to use your own work-related projects.

At the end of each chapter is a summary of operations covered in that chapter. These summaries are intentionally brief and meant to be memory-joggers. For a more complete discussion, you should refer to the material in the chapter itself.

Here is a chapter-by-chapter description of what is covered in this book.

Chapter 1 covers loading the MultiMate program into an IBM PC with dual disk drives and using a document-storage disk. It also orients you to the keyboard, the Main Menu, and the Help facility.

Chapter 2 shows you how to create a new document and explains in detail all of the information you see on the screen displays from the moment you leave the Main Menu until you arrive at the first screen of a document. Discussions of typing on the keyboard using wraparound and exiting a document finish off the chapter.

Chapter 3 introduces basic functions that allow you to control the cursor so you may rapidly move from one spot in the document to another.

In *Chapter 4* you learn about editing features—those that make correcting errors so easy—and about saving your document to disk.

Chapter 5 compares formatting with MultiMate to formatting with a typewriter. It also includes everything you ever wanted to know about format lines but were afraid to ask.

Chapter 6 discusses advanced formatting functions.

Chapter 7 discusses *special features,* including Center, Indent, Hardspace, soft and hard hyphens, Underline/Deunderline, and Super/Subscript.

In *Chapter 8* and *Chapter 9* you will learn how to print a document and how to use other printing features supported by MultiMate.

Chapter 10 and *Chapter 11* cover the advanced editing functions that allow relocation and automatic replacement of text: Move, Copy, External Copy, and Search and Replace. Format line replace is also covered.

Chapter 12 explains use of the Library function, with which you can store and recall repeated words and phrases and *boilerplate* material (standard paragraphs).

Chapter 13 explains the Merge function, which is used for creating personalized form letters.

Chapter 14 examines the use of headers and footers for page numbering, and *Chapter 15* covers the column manipulation functions Insert, Delete, Move and Copy.

Chapter 16 covers the document handling utilities: Copy a Document, Move a Document, Rename a Document, etc., that are accessible from the main menu. This chapter also shows you how to print or search the document summary screens.

Chapter 17 and *Chapter 18* explain Key Procedures and the Spell Check/Spell Edit features. These features are enhancements to version 3.20 and later versions.

Appendix A covers other utilities, and Appendix B covers MultiMate key combinations for the IBM personal computer.

What You Need to Begin

To use this book for a hands-on experience, you will need a MultiMate *system disk* and a *formatted document-storage disk.*

This book is not intended to replace *MultiMate Word Processing for the IBM PC,* the manual published by MultiMate International Corporation which came with your program. You should refer to this manual for details on backing up your word processing system disk and preparing your document-storage disk. You should also consult it for information on how to load MultiMate if you are using a system other than an IBM PC with dual disk drives. The manual also explains how to apply the optional keyboard labels which identify the keys by their MultiMate functions.

A Note to Teachers

A supplementary *Instructor's Manual* of approximately 100 pages is available for those who are interested in using this book as a textbook. *The Instructor's Manual* suggests various teaching schedules, outlines teaching techniques that have worked for me, provides supplementary exercises which you are free to duplicate for your classes, and presents a hard copy of material that can be stored on students' document-storage disks for them to recall and edit. Send your name and address and $20 (to cover the costs of photocopying, handling, and postage) to *MultiMate Instructor's Manual,* 18314 - 48 Avenue West, Lynnwood, WA 98037.

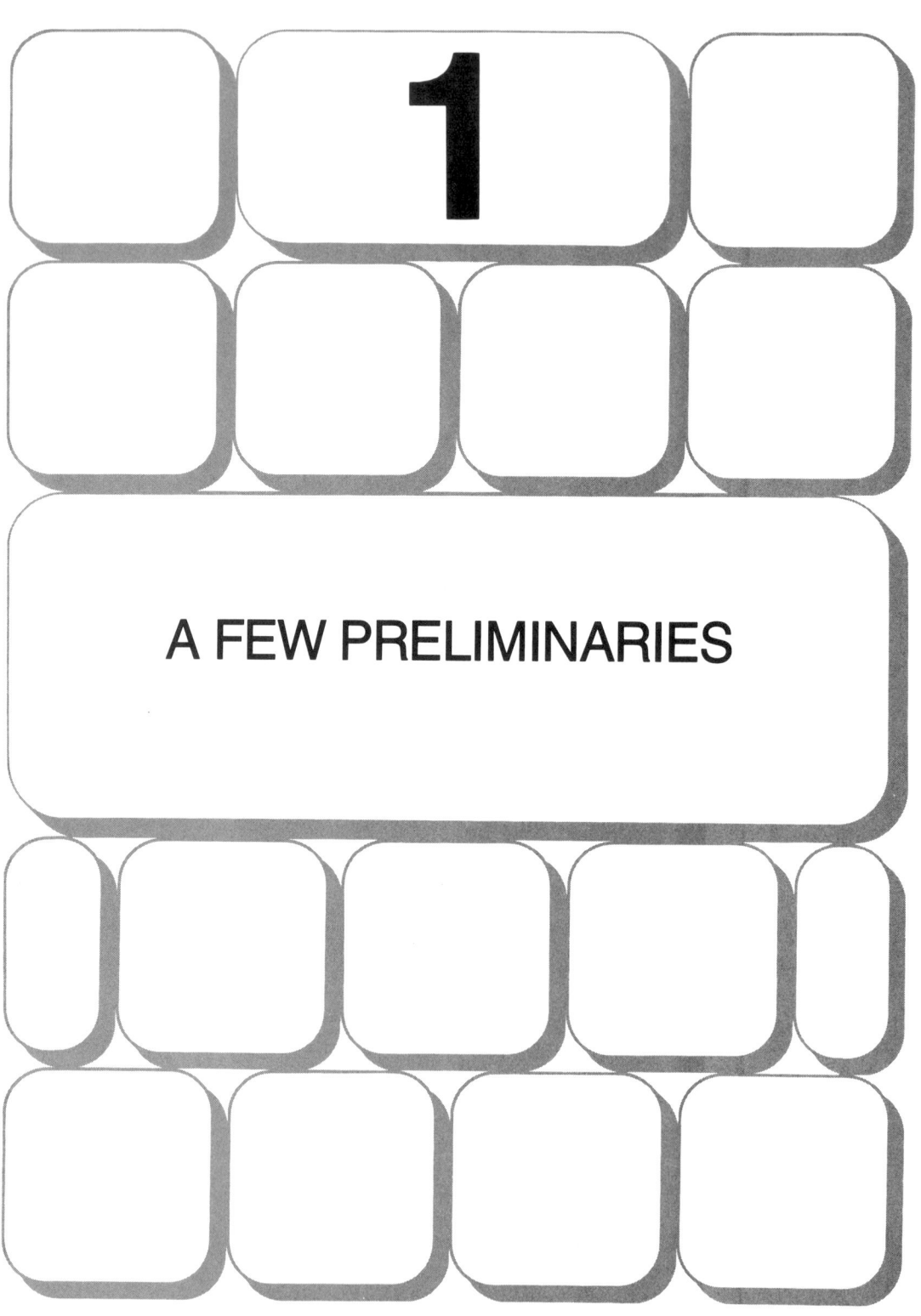

1

A FEW PRELIMINARIES

THE KEYBOARD

In this chapter, we'll examine the keys you will use with MultiMate. You will first learn the symbol on the keyboard, then the function of each key. Remember that this information is specific to MultiMate. Don't expect the keys to behave in exactly the same way when you are using a different program.

One unique feature of this keyboard is that all keys will repeat if held down. Because of this, you may need to develop a slightly lighter touch when you type. If an operation doesn't work properly, repeat the steps and be careful to tap the keys quickly and lightly.

Let's look at how the keys function. Refer to Figure 1.1 as you read through the following explanations.

Figure 1.1 – IBM PC keyboard

Special Function Keys (F1–F10)

Ten special *function keys,* F1–F10, are located at the left of the keyboard. MultiMate uses these special function keys to perform various operations. They can be used alone or with the shift, Alt, and Ctrl keys. When you are instructed to press F6, be sure to use the single key with *F6* on it; don't type an *F* and then a 6.

Alternate (Alt) and Control (Ctrl) Keys

Alt and Ctrl are always used with another key to perform special functions or to change the effect of the key they are used with. For example, you know that tapping *s* while holding down the shift key will make an *S*. If you hold Alt down while tapping *s,* you will create a *required space* (a space that will never be converted to a return during wraparound). Just like the shift key, you must hold Alt and Ctrl down *while* you tap another key.

Escape Key (Esc)

The escape key is located to the left of the 1 in the top row of numbers. If you make an error in the middle of an operation, Esc allows you to restore the text to its original condition.

Letter and Number/Symbol Keys

These keys are used like those on a regular typewriter with one exception: numbers and letters are different to the computer. For example, you cannot use a lowercase *L* for the number *one,* or a capital *O* for *zero.* You will be able to tell the difference between the *O* and the *zero* on the screen because the zero looks like this: ϕ.

Numeric Key Pad

On the right side of the keyboard, you will see a numeric key pad. Although you may use these keys to type numbers, it is not advisable.

A Few Preliminaries **3**

Whenever you are instructed to press a number, use the numbers in the top row above the letter keys.

Shift Keys (⇧)

The two shift keys at either end of the bottom row of typewriter keys have a hollow arrow (⇧) on them. As on a typewriter, you hold them down while you press another key. If a key has two characters on it, you access the top character by holding shift down while tapping the key. The shift keys are most often used for typing capital letters.

With MultiMate, the shift keys are also used with the special function keys, F1–F10. These functions will be covered in later sections.

Space Bar

As on a typewriter, a tap on the space bar on your computer keyboard leaves a blank space between characters. The space bar is the wide key below the letter keys; it has no markings on it.

On a typewriter you can space under characters without affecting them. When you use MultiMate, however, the space bar *destroys characters*. This means that if your *cursor* (the small blinking light on the screen) is under a character when you press the space bar, that character will be replaced by a blank space.

Note: Remember that a space is a character. Do not use the space bar to move the cursor. If you do, you will replace all the existing characters along the way with spaces!

Spaces can be made to show up on the monitor as dots if you wish. See the directions for doing this in the section on permanently changing the document and system defaults in Appendix A.

Tab/Backtab Key (⇆)

The tab/backtab key has double arrows (⇆) on it. It is located just to the left of the letter Q. Just as on a typewriter, pressing tab will jump you to the next tab stop that has been set. In MultiMate, whenever you press tab, you will see this symbol: >>.

When you hold down shift while pressing tab, you activate the backtab function, which moves you to the beginning of the line on which your cursor is resting. No symbol appears on the screen when you use backtab.

Return Key (←⏎)

The return key is marked with a broken arrow (←⏎); it is located just to the left of the numeric keypad. This key moves your cursor down one line and to the left edge of the line. (This movement parallels the direction of the arrow: down and to the left.) *Note: The return key produces a character. If your cursor is resting under a character when you press return, that character will be replaced by the return symbol:* <<.

Return is also used with other keys to execute certain functions. In some operations, you press return as the final keystroke, so at times the return key functions as an *enter key*.

Capitals Lock Key (Caps Lock)

The Caps Lock key is located to the right of the space bar. Like the shift lock on a typewriter, Caps Lock is used to make continuous uppercase letters. However, Caps Lock *does not* activate the symbols on the top half of the number keys. To activate the upper symbols, hold down shift and press the appropriate number key.

Caps Lock is called a *toggle* key. Press it once and it's on continuously; press it again and it's off. Caps Lock has been activated if you see S:↑ in the lower right-hand corner of the screen. Caps Lock is off if the arrow points down (S:↓).

If Caps Lock is on and you press shift and a letter, you will produce a lowercase letter. Check to see if Caps Lock is on before you press shift.

Number Lock Key (Num Lock)

Num Lock lets you access the numbers on the numeric keypad. When using MultiMate, you will want Num Lock off.

Num Lock is a toggle key. It is on when the lower right hand corner of the screen shows an *N:↑* and it is off when you see an *N:↓*.

Cursor-Moving Keys

The *cursor* is the blinking light which shows your present location on the screen. This is the place where the next character will be entered or the next operation will begin.

There are four keys on the numeric keypad used to move the cursor one space at a time to any part of the screen. These four keys have both a number and an arrow on them (e.g. 2 and ↓). The arrows indicate the direction the cursor will move. Collectively, they will be identified as the *cursor-moving keys;* individually, as the *left cursor mover, right cursor mover, up cursor mover,* and *down cursor mover.*

These cursor-moving keys are different from the space bar because they allow you to move your cursor under characters *without destroying them.* Remember to use these keys, not the space bar, to move the cursor to a new location.

Backspace Key (←)

The backspace key has a left arrow (←) on it. It is located above the return key. The backspace moves your cursor one space to the left. If you press backspace when you are already at the far left edge of the writing line, you will move to the right end of the previous line. Like all computer keys, the backspace key repeats; it will continue as long as you hold it down.

You can choose to set the backspace key either to remove characters or to move under characters without destroying them. See the directions in Appendix A, in the section on permanently changing the document and system defaults.

Other Keys

The specialized functions of other keys will be fully explained in later chapters. The key labelled *Scroll Lock* is not used with Multi-Mate.

INSERTING DISKS INTO DRIVES

In an IBM PC with horizontal disk drives, the drive on the left is called drive A and the one on the right, drive B.

After you have copied and backed up the original disks you received from MultiMate International, insert the copy of the MultiMate system disk into drive A and close the drive door.

Next, insert a formatted disk on which you want to store documents into drive B and close the drive door. Detailed disk formatting instructions are given in the MultiMate user manual.

At this point the disks are in the disk drives, but nothing has yet been loaded into the computer's memory.

LOADING DOS AND MULTIMATE

There are two ways to load a copy of the information on the MultiMate system disk into an IBM PC with dual disk drives.

1. If the computer is turned off and the system disk is in drive A (the disk drive on the left side), close the drive doors and turn on the computer. The DOS (Disk Operating System) will begin to load automatically.

2. If the computer is already on and your system disk is in drive A, close the drive doors, and hold down Ctrl-Alt while you tap the key labeled Del. Release the three keys; the DOS begins to load.

In both of these methods, you should hear a whirring noise and see the red light on the front of the drive go on. *Note: Do not open a drive door when the red light is on*—this could damage the disk, the disk drive, or both.

Depending on whether your computer is on or off, use one of the two procedures now to load your MultiMate system disk. Figure 1.2 shows what the first screen displays.

This screen display indicates that the DOS is being loaded. You will then be prompted to indicate the date and time.

You may indicate the date in any of the following ways: 4/21/84, 4/21/1984, 4-21-84, or 4-21-1984. (Remember not to type in the day of the week and to use only numbers i.e., no lowercase *L* for a *one*.)

If you don't wish to enter a date, press return when the cursor waits after the word *Date*. However, you should take the time to enter the date because then your documents will be dated automatically for you.

After you have entered the date, press return. The time that has been set is then displayed. If you want to change that time, enter the numbers for the hour, minute, second, and half second (if desired) separated by colons. Use 24-hour military time. 4 p.m., for example, would be 16:00:00. (Remember to use the numbers above the letter keys.) After entering the time, press return. If you do not wish to record the time, just press return.

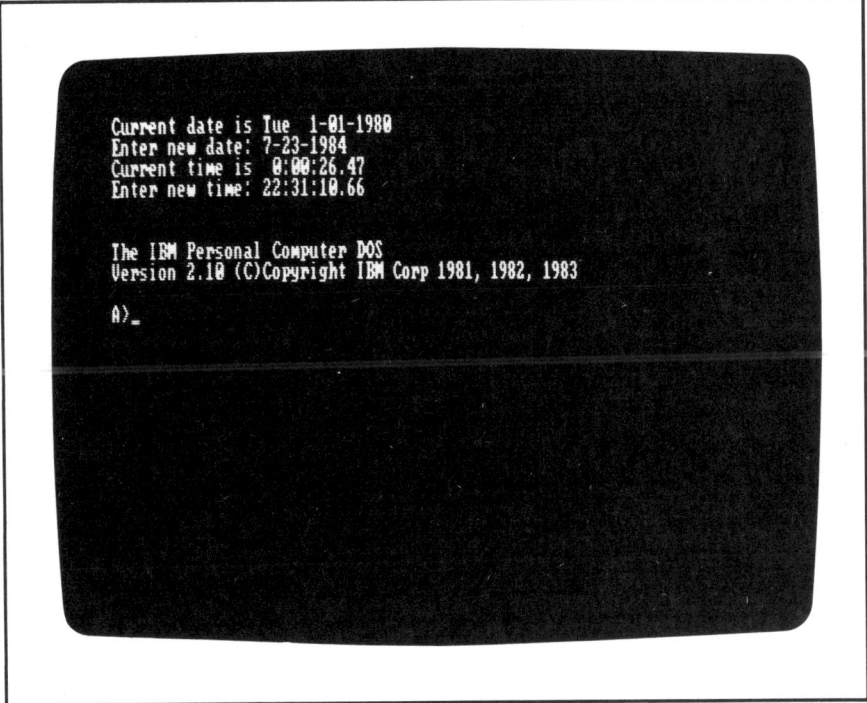

Figure 1.2 – First screen display

You will know the DOS (Disk Operating System) has been loaded when the *A Prompt* (A>) is on the screen and the cursor appears after it. Type *WP* (either upper- or lowercase) and press return. A copy of the MultiMate program will be loaded from the program disk into the computer's memory.

When the program has finished loading, the MultiMate *title screen* appears. As shown in Figure 1.3, this screen displays the title of the program and copyright information. The screen prompt instructs you to press the space bar. When you do so, the next thing you see is the Main Menu.

THE MAIN MENU

The MultiMate Main Menu shown in Figure 1.4 displays all the choices of operations you have. You will learn about each of these in later chapters.

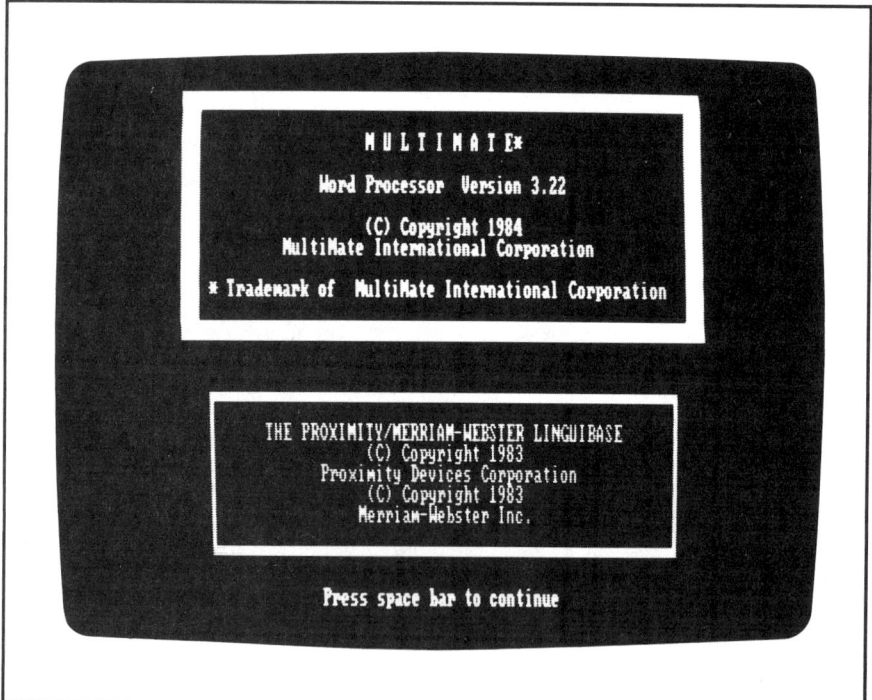

Figure 1.3 – MultiMate title screen

The cursor rests on the space after the words *DESIRED FUNC-TION*. The system is now ready for you to indicate your choice. Before doing so, however, let's look at a couple of other features. Notice the message which is under the words *DESIRED FUNCTION*. It is called an *on-screen prompt*.

ON-SCREEN PROMPTS

A very helpful feature of MultiMate is the use of prompts on the screen. These prompts guide you through the steps of an operation and also let you know when you have done something inappropriate. These prompts will appear at various locations on the screen.

The on-screen prompt below the Main Menu tells you exactly what to do: *Enter the number of the function; press RETURN*. In Chapter 2, you will begin to explore all of the Main Menu options in detail, but first, let's take a look at the Help facility.

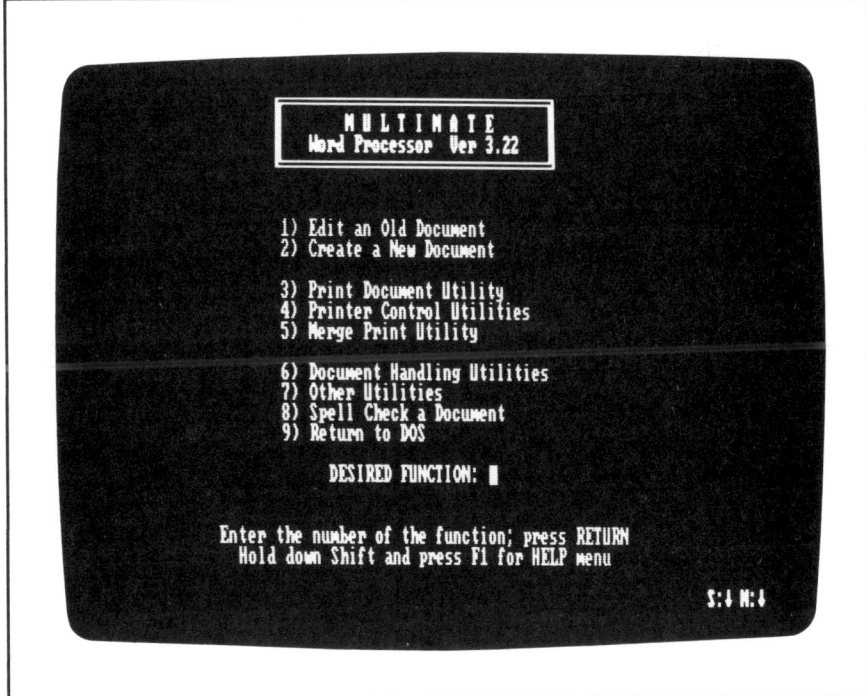

Figure 1.4 – MultiMate Main Menu

THE HELP FACILITY

One of the most useful features of MultiMate is its extensive and easily accessed Help facility, which gives you information about all MultiMate functions. From either the Main Menu or from within a document, just press shift-F1 (at the same time) to display the Help menu screen. You will now see the screen in Figure 1.5.

You can call up any of the specialized Help submenus on the general topics shown by pressing the appropriate number. If you don't know the category of help you need, press 6 for a list of *all* the available Help topics and the keys which access them.

Press 6 now to display the list of topics for which help is available. It will tell you which key to use for a particular function. You can *scroll* through this list to see more topics by pressing the space bar.

This alphabetic list is moved up one line on the screen each time you press the space bar, and it will repeat if you continue to press

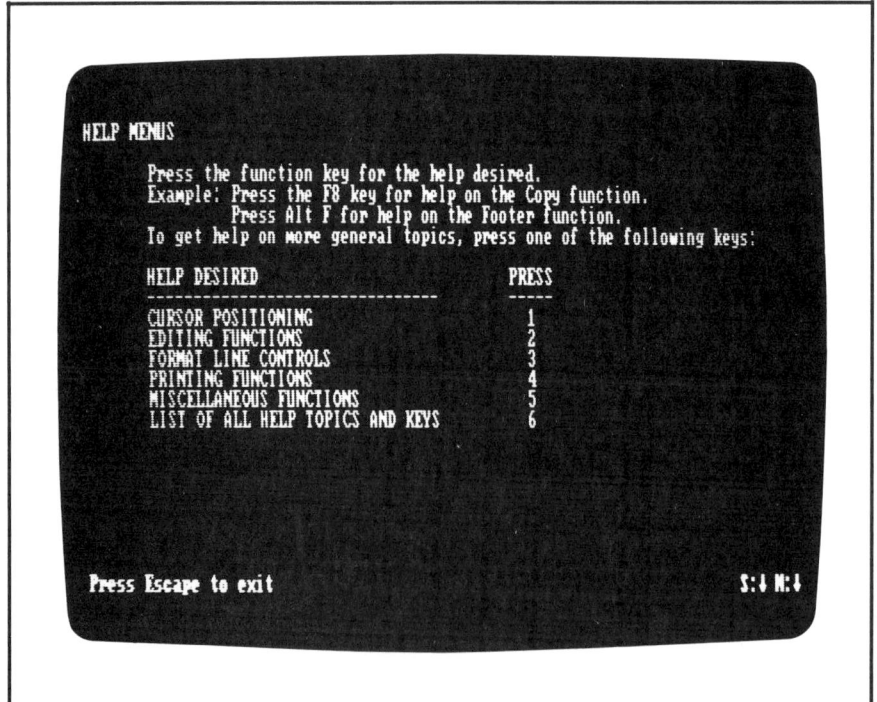

Figure 1.5 – Help menu

the space bar. You will learn about each of these features in this book. For now, just remember shift-F1 brings the Help menu to the screen.

Now take a look at the kind of detailed help you can get from within the Help facility. If you need more extensive help, such as information about what a function accomplishes or where the cursor should be before a function is begun, press the key listed after the name of the function on the list entitled *LIST OF ALL HELP TOPICS AND KEYS*. For example, if you forget what the return key is used for, you should type an R. You will then see the information that is displayed in Figure 1.6, the six uses of return.

To exit the Help facility, press Esc to return to the Main Menu.

If you want to stop your work with MultiMate for now, simply remove the disks. It's a good idea to have the Main Menu displayed on the screen before you remove the disks to be sure all operations have been completed.

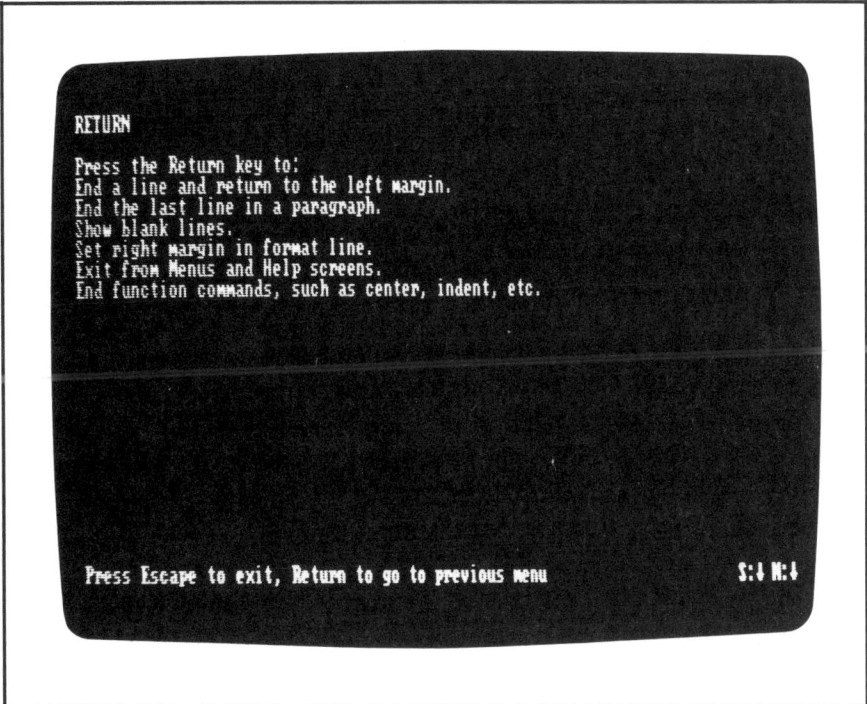

Figure 1.6 – Return key Help screen

If you want to continue, turn to Chapter 2, where you will learn how to create a document.

SUMMARY OF OPERATIONS COVERED IN THIS CHAPTER

Loading MultiMate When the Computer is Off

1. Put the MultiMate system disk in drive A and close the drive door.
2. Put a formatted document-storage disk in drive B and close the drive door.
3. Turn the computer on.
4. Wait until DOS is loaded and the system prompt (A >) is displayed.
5. Enter the date and time (if you wish), and press return after each.
6. Type *WP* and press return.

Loading MultiMate When the Computer is On

1. Put the MultiMate system disk in drive A and close the door.
2. Put a formatted document-storage disk in drive B and close the door.
3. Hold Ctrl and Alt down while you press Del. Release all three keys at once.
4. Wait until DOS is loaded and the system prompt (A >) is displayed.
5. Enter the date and time (if you wish), and press return after each.
6. Type *WP* and tap return.

Accessing a Main Menu Function When the Main Menu Is on the Screen

1. Type the number of the desired option and press return.

Accessing/Exiting the Help Facility from the Main Menu or from within a Document

1. Press shift-F1 to access a list of the Help menus.
2. Indicate the kind of help you want by pressing the number indicated on the list. If you know the key used for the function with which you need help, press it. If you don't know which key to press, tap 6 for a list of all Help topics and keys.
3. Press Esc to exit the Help facility; the cursor will return to the location from which you started.

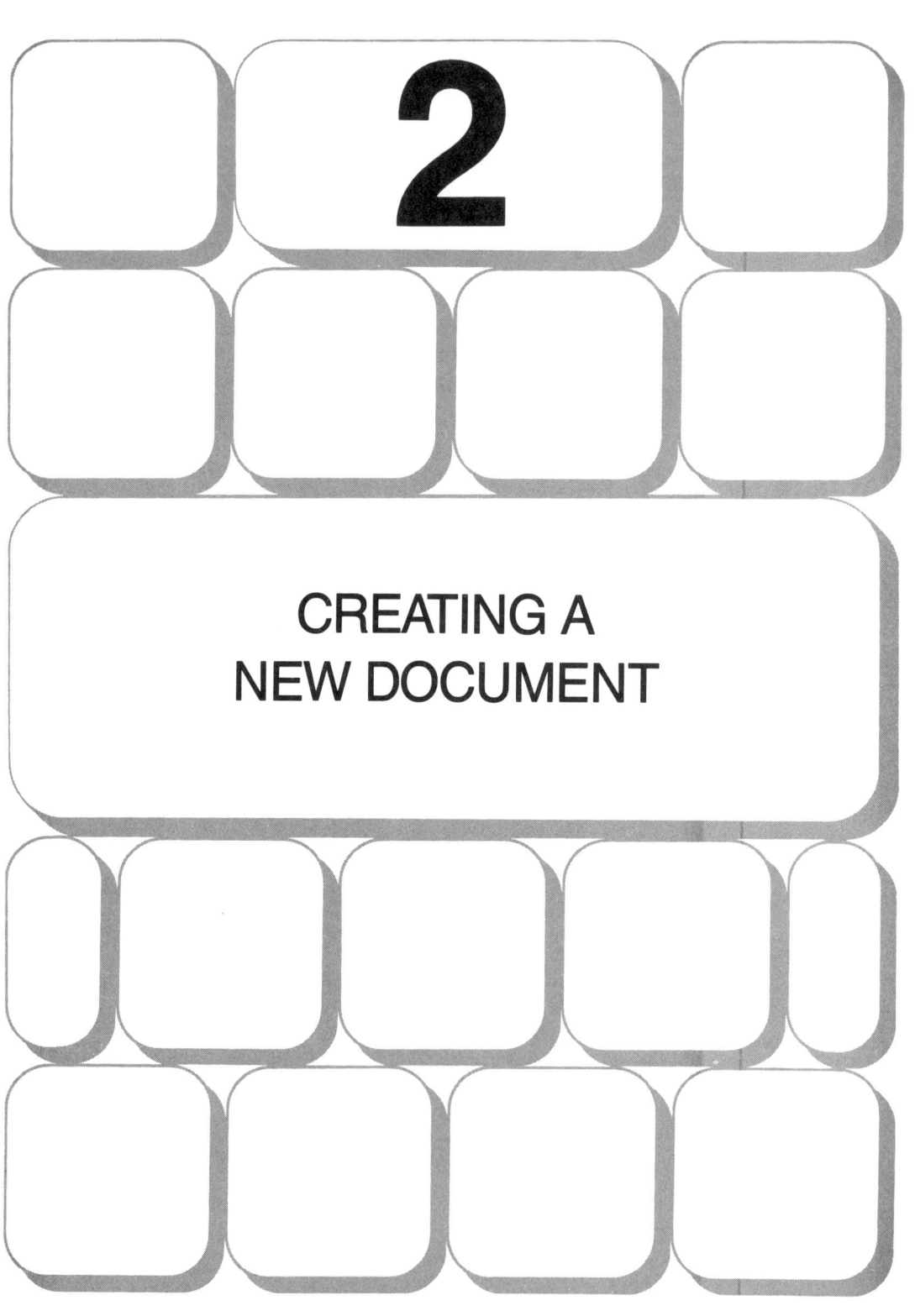

With your MultiMate program disk and document-storage disk in the computer and the Main Menu on the screen, you are ready to begin the process of creating a new document. The screen prompt instructs you to *Enter the number of the function; press RETURN.* So, to indicate that you are ready to create a new document, type 2 and press return.

THE CREATE A NEW DOCUMENT SCREEN

After you type 2 and press return, a new screen appears, as illustrated in Figure 2.1.

Let's take a look at this screen. On the left, the word *Drive:* is followed by a letter. This tells you on which drive your document will be stored. If you are using a system with two disk drives, the letter is

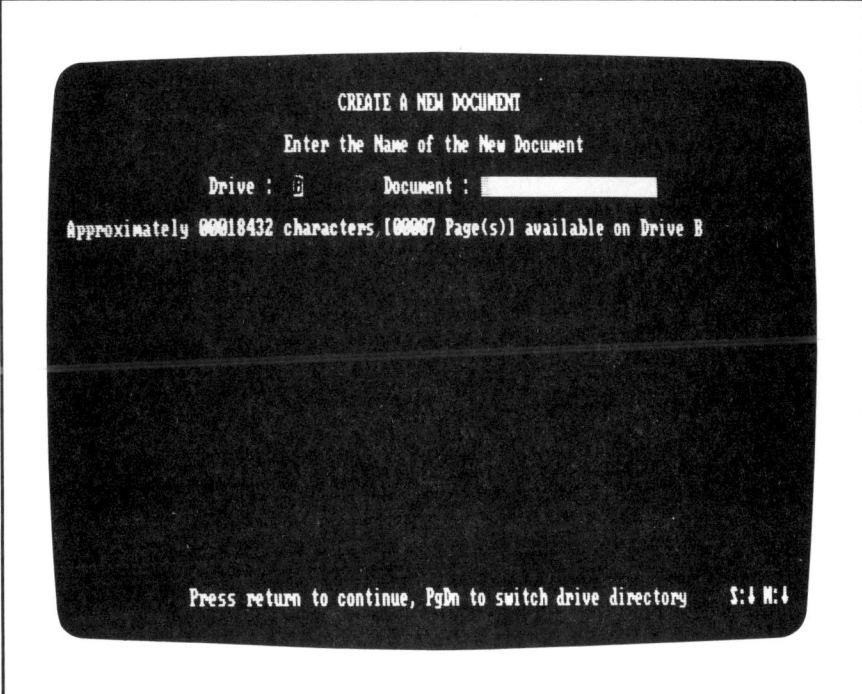

Figure 2.1 – Create a New Document screen

probably B. It is best to store documents on the disk in drive B if you have a computer with dual drives.

A condition which is preset in the program is called a *default*. The letter *B* after *Drive:* tells you that MultiMate will by default store documents on the disk in drive B. MultiMate defaults can be permanently changed as you will learn in later chapters.

Defaults can also be temporarily changed just for the document you are currently working on. For example, if you wanted your document stored on the disk in drive A (on the same disk as your MultiMate program), backspace to move the cursor under the letter after *Drive:* and then change that letter to *A*. Let's use the default setting for this document.

Next, you will see a line which tells you how many characters and pages are available on the disk currently housed in the selected drive.

The next area below is the *drive directory,* an alphabetic list of all the documents already on the disk. It shows the first eight characters of the name of each document. If the disk is unused, no document names will appear at this time. To view the drive directory of the disk in the other drive, press the PgDn key located on the numeric keypad. Press PgDn now and notice how much room is left on the disk in drive A for documents.

The cursor should now be resting after the word *Document:* . This is where you will type the name of your new document. If a name already appears in the blank after *Document:*, you can type the new name over it. If the new document name is shorter, you can delete the extra characters with the Del key located below the numeric keypad.

A document name

- should indicate to you the contents of the document,

- can contain up to 20 letters or numbers (although only the first eight will appear in the drive directory),

- should avoid all punctuation and spaces, and

- should not be a name that has been used for another document in the same directory. At least one of the first eight characters must be different or the system will tell you *SORRY . . . DOCUMENT ALREADY EXISTS.*

FIRSTDOC would fit all of those characteristics, so that's what you should now type in the blank. Then, as indicated on the screen, press return. Whether you type upper- or lowercase letters, the names in the drive directory will automatically appear in all capital letters.

THE DOCUMENT SUMMARY SCREEN

Now you will see the screen in Figure 2.2. This is the Document Summary Screen which contains information such as the author, operator, creation date, etc. A Document Summary Screen is stored with each document you create. You can search through these screens later to find information about your document. In Chapter 16, you will learn more about this operation.

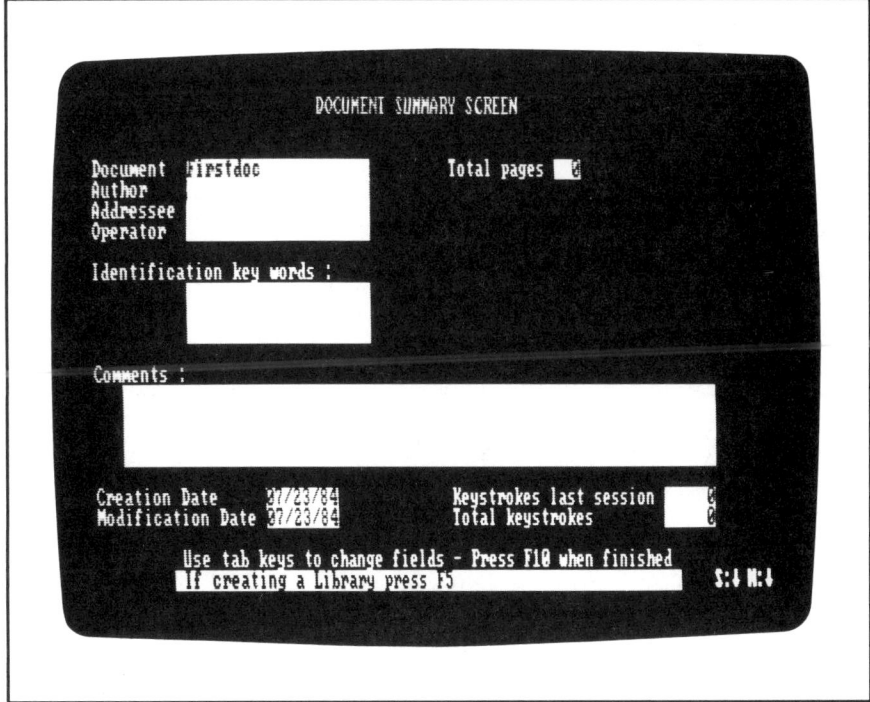

Figure 2.2 – Document Summary Screen

Read the information at the bottom of the screen. It tells you how to move around on the screen and what to do when you are finished:

Use tab keys to change fields—Press F10 when finished.

To advance from one section to another, use the tab key. If you did not wish to add information to this summary screen, you could immediately press F10, as the screen prompt indicates.

For now, press tab to advance to each of the fields described below.

Document The name you gave this document on the previous screen automatically appears here. It should say *FIRSTDOC* now. Press tab to move down the screen.

Author If you are are typing the document for someone else, type his or her name here. Type Carol Holcomb Dreger in the blank after *Author*. Since that name used every available space in this field, it is not necessary to press tab. The cursor will automatically advance to the next field.

Addressee If you were creating a letter or memo, you would type the name of the person to whom it is addressed here. This document will not be sent to anyone, so leave this line blank and tab to the next area.

Operator Type your name here—you are now the word processing operator! Press tab to move to the next field.

Identification Key Words In this space you could indicate the type of letter or document this is (for example, a collection letter, a sales letter, a proposal, etc.). You could also remind yourself of the type of business the addressee is in, or indicate any key words you might want to use when searching through your files later. Since this document won't be needed for long, type *temporary* on the line. Tab to the next section.

Comments In this section, type special notes to yourself. For example, you could write the name of a *Library* which you used to create the document (you'll learn about Libraries in Chapter 12) or a reminder about special paper on which the document should be printed, etc. Type *use pink letterhead* on the line. Now examine the rest of the Document Summary Screen.

Creation Date When you first loaded the MultiMate program, you should have entered the current date. The date on which you are creating this document will automatically appear here because you entered it at that time. If you didn't enter the date, a default date was entered by the system.

Modification Date If you return to this document at another time to revise it or look it over, the date on which the document was last entered will appear in this area.

The creation and modification dates help you determine which version of a much-revised document you have before you.

Keystrokes last session If you are editing a document, the number after the heading tells you how many keys were pressed the last time the document was entered. For example, if you were correcting errors in the document and the correction took three keystrokes, 3 would appear here.

Total keystrokes If you had already created a document, the number following this heading would indicate the total number of keystrokes in the document. This information could be important if you typically create very long documents. MultiMate has a limit of 6,144 characters per page and of 250 pages per document. This means your document may not exceed 1,536,000 characters. If it does, you may get an error message, and lose some or all of your document.

When you are finished with this Document Summary Screen, follow the screen prompt and press F10. You now see the Modify Document Defaults screen, shown in Figure 2.3.

THE MODIFY DOCUMENT DEFAULTS SCREEN

The Modify Document Defaults screen allows you to specify the characteristics of this document in the following areas. Here is an explanation of each area.

Allow widows and orphans? Widows and orphans are single lines of a paragraph either at the beginning or the end of a page. According to standard typing rules, a single line of a paragraph

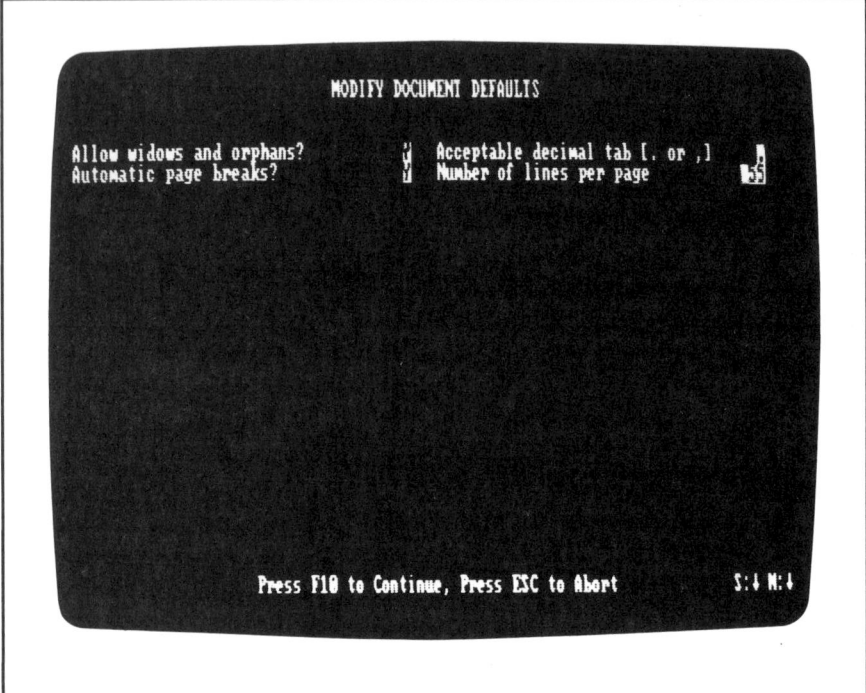

Figure 2.3 – Modify Document Defaults screen

should never be left alone at the bottom of one page or carried over to the top of the next page. If you type *N* here, the program will adhere to that rule. If you type *Y* here, widows and orphans will be permitted when the system automatically creates new pages. If a *Y* does not appear here, type one now.

Automatic page breaks? If you type *N* here, you will have to press F2 every time you wish to create a new page. If you type *Y*, MultiMate will automatically begin a new page when the number of lines per page you specify is reached. If a *Y* does not appear here, type one now.

Acceptable decimal tab [. or ,] If you are typing a column of numbers with a decimal tab, you can choose to line up numbers around the comma or the decimal point. Typing a period will align numbers at the decimal point; typing a comma will align numbers at the commas. If a decimal does not appear here, type one using the period key.

Number of lines per page You can select any number of lines per page from 1 to 150. Standard 8½ by 11-inch paper will allow printing of 66 lines (at a standard 6 horizontal lines per inch). If you choose a higher number you won't be able to print your document on standard-sized paper. If you answered Y to *Automatic page breaks?* the system will create a new page every time it reaches the number of lines specified here. If you answered N, then the system will just light up the line number in the status line (and possibly beep) when the line number of the preset page length is reached. Type *55* if another number appears in the blank.

After you have finished looking at the Modify Document Defaults screen, follow the screen prompt. It tells you to press F10 to continue on to the first screen of the document.

THE STATUS LINE

The first line you see at the top of this and every screen of a document is called a *status line*. It shows the name of the document, the page of the document you are presently on, and a line number and column number which indicate the present location of the cursor. A sample status line is shown in Figure 2.4.

THE FORMAT LINE

Immediately under the *status line* is the *format line*. It shows vertical spacing, tab stops, and the length of the writing line. This particular format line is called a *system default format* line because it is preset and automatically appears on the first screen of a new document.

The system default format line has the following characteristics:

- single spacing (indicated by the *1* at the left side of the screen)
- tab stops set at 5, 10, and 15 (indicated by the tab symbol: ≫)
- a 75-space writing line (indicated by the return symbol: ≪)

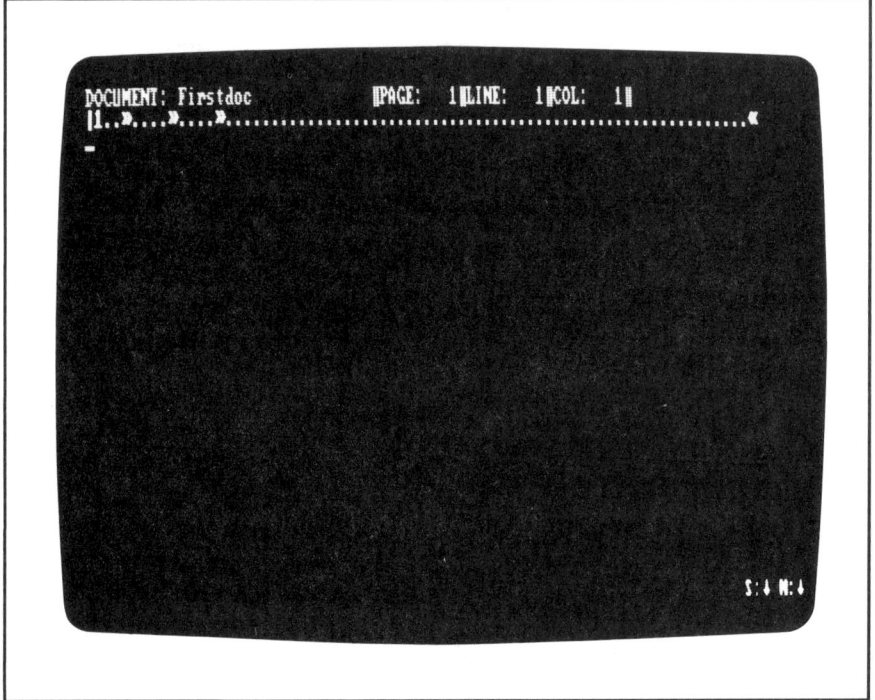

Figure 2.4 – Status line

The system default format line is illustrated in Figure 2.5.

If these are not the spacing, tabs, and line length you will be using most often, you can permanently change the system default format line. You can also change a format line just for the document on which you are working. You will learn how to make these changes in later chapters.

WORD WRAP

When you use a typewriter, you must press return at the end of each line. When you type on a word processor, you don't have to use the return key at the end of every line because word processors have a feature called *word wrap* or *wraparound*.

Word processors are programmed to fit as many words as possible on a line. If a word can't fit on a line, it is automatically moved

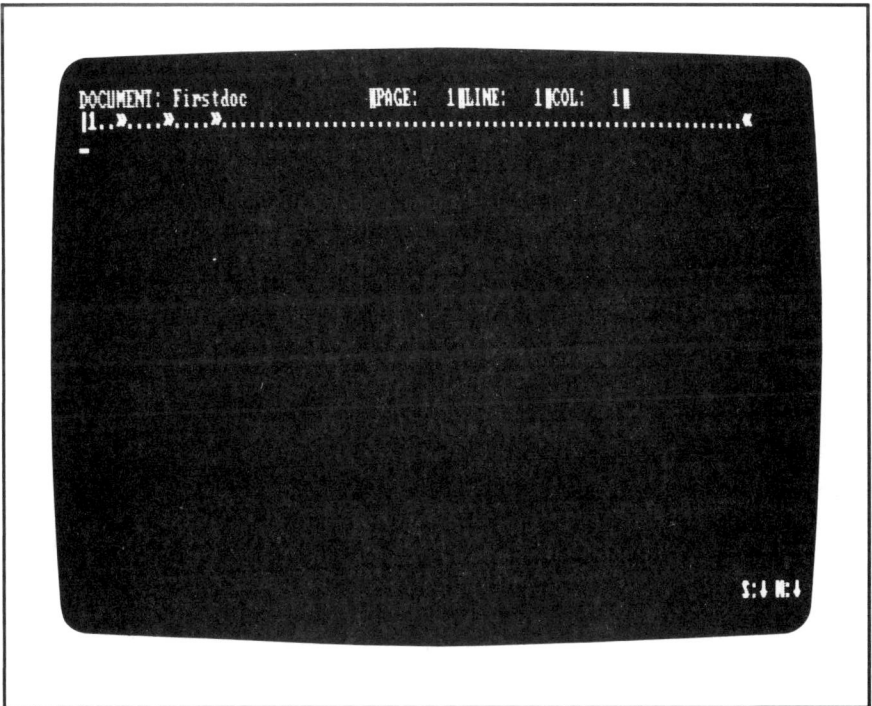

Figure 2.5 – System default format line

(wrapped around) to the next line as soon as you type one character more than the writing line length that has been set in the format line. This automatic return feature is one reason you are usually able to type faster on a word processor than on a typewriter.

Note: You must be very careful to notice where your cursor is located before you type a character. Whenever you press return, the symbol ≪ appears on the screen. Since this symbol represents a character, it will be replaced if you press another character (such as a letter) when the cursor is under the return symbol (≪). When you do replace or delete a return, the text following it immediately moves up to take its place.

As you type the text below, watch what happens when you type the last word in the sentence. Press tab when you see ≫; press return when you see ≪.

>>This sentence was typed with the word processing feature known as wraparound. ≪

You don't have to press return at the end of every line of text. Instead, use return to:

- end a short line of typing that doesn't reach the right end of the writing line. This will move the cursor to the left edge of the writing line and one line lower on the screen.

- end the last line of a paragraph in order to create a new paragraph.

- leave a line completely blank (in this case the ≪ symbol will appear at the left edge of the writing line).

EXITING THE DOCUMENT

Once you have finished with a document, there are three ways to exit it.

The most direct way for you to exit the document and save it on a disk is to press F10 when your cursor is in the document. You will be returned to the Main Menu, and the document will be saved to the disk. F10 is called the Save/Exit key.

Another way to exit the document you are currently in is to go directly to any other Main Menu function. To do this, press Alt plus the number of a Main Menu function. (For example, Alt-3 would access the printing function.) The document is automatically saved to the disk when the new function begins.

A third way to exit the document is to press the Esc key. The question *Do you wish to escape without saving this page? (Y/N)* appears. If you type Y, you will be returned to the Main Menu and the document page you are presently on will not be saved. If your page had not previously been saved, it would be gone forever. However, MultiMate automatically saves the current page to disk when you:

- move to another page (i.e. press F2 to create a page break manually or have one occur automatically because of defaults that were set)

- access any Main Menu function directly from a document with Alt and the function number

- press shift-F10

- press F10

If you had previously saved the page to disk, the original would still exist on the disk and only this latest revision would be lost when you typed Y.

Note: When you recall a document from disk, you are actually recalling a *copy* of it into memory; the original remains on the disk. When you store a document to disk after revising it, the revised document replaces the original.

Incidentally, if you type N to answer the question, *Do you wish to escape without saving this page? (Y/N),* the page will be saved to the disk and you will remain in the document.

You should now save *FIRSTDOC* to disk by pressing the Save/Exit key, F10. The Main Menu will then appear on the screen.

REMOVING THE DISKS FROM THE DISK DRIVES

Before you remove the disks from the disk drives or turn the system off, you will want to be certain that the text of a document you are working on is saved to disk and that no operation is stopped midstream. For these reasons, you should always have the Main Menu displayed on the screen before you remove the disks.

AN OPPORTUNITY TO PRACTICE

To practice creating a new document and using wraparound, type the following document. You will need this document to practice several other functions introduced in the next chapter and in later chapters. Follow these directions:

1. From the Main Menu, create a new document named *PRACTICE.* Follow the screen prompts to get to the first screen of the document. On the Modify Document Defaults screen use the following settings:

    Allow widows and orphans? Y
    Automatic page breaks? N
    Acceptable decimal tab [. or ,] .
    Number of lines per page? 55

Then fill in the Document Summary Screen.

2. Type the following material using the system default format line. You can activate Caps Lock to type several capitalized characters in a row.

    Use single spacing with double spaces (one blank line) between the paragraphs. Don't indent the first lines of the paragraphs. *Note:* Your lines may end in different places than the ones here.

    If you make errors, ignore them for now. In Chapter 4 you will learn the most efficient ways to correct your errors.

QUALITIES OF SUCCESSFUL WP OPERATORS

Word processing involves more than just new-fangled office equipment; wp is concept encompassing procedures and people as well as equipment. Since the equipment usually gets most of the attention, this article is concerned with the wp operator. What are the qualities of a successful wp operator?

POSITIVE ATTITUDE: Only with a positive attitude toward change, an eagerness to learn computerized equipment, and a delight in challenges can person overcome the frustrating moments and possess the discipline and dedication to keep up with this fast-changing field.

EFFICIENT, WELL-ORGANIZED, ABLE TO WORK UNDER PRESSURE: Successful wp operators must manage their time well, prioritize jobs appropriately, and organize electronic files for efficient retrieval. They need to grasp concepts and verbal directions quickly and are often expected to do their best work under pressure.

UNDERSTANDING OF AND BELIEF IN TEAMWORK: Since at least two (and sometimes several) people are involved in the production of a final document, the wp operator must be able to work as a member of a team whose goal is a quality finished product. At the same time, pride in one's own work is necessary to guarantee that each step of the process is done well.

GENERAL INTELLIGENCE AND BUSINESS SENSE: Efficient wp operators must be able to memorize codes and, even more importantly, be able to "think like the equipment"—to know what it can and can't (will and won't) do if a specific function is activated. Word processing activities also involve decision-making, initiative, common sense, and knowledge of acceptable business procedures and standards.

DOCUMENT PREPARATION SKILLS: These include not only keyboarding skills, but also visualization and planning skills used to format the finished document (i.e. determine margins, tabs, type size and style, line spacing, length, etc.). Excellent spelling, grammar, punctuation, and proofreading skills are also essential.

This may sound like a big order, but remember these two things: (1) a word processing system will perform only as well as the person who operates it, and (2) not every speedy typist has the other qualities required to be a successful word processing operator!

3. After the document is typed, leave it on the screen and turn to Chapter 3.

SUMMARY OF OPERATIONS COVERED IN THIS CHAPTER

Create a New Document

1. With the Main Menu on the screen, type 2 and press return.
2. Type in the name of the document and press return.
3. Fill in as much of the Document Summary Screen as necessary.
4. Press F10.
5. Reset any items on the Modify Document Defaults screen.
6. Press F10.
7. The cursor will be on the first screen of the document.

Save and Exit the Document to Return to the Main Menu

1. Press F10.

Exit the Document Directly to Another Main Menu Function

1. From within the document hold down the Alt key and type the number of the desired Main Menu function.
2. The document is automatically saved to disk. The cursor will be on the first screen of the desired function.

Exit the Document without Saving the Current Page

1. Press Esc.
2. Answer the prompt question by typing Y.

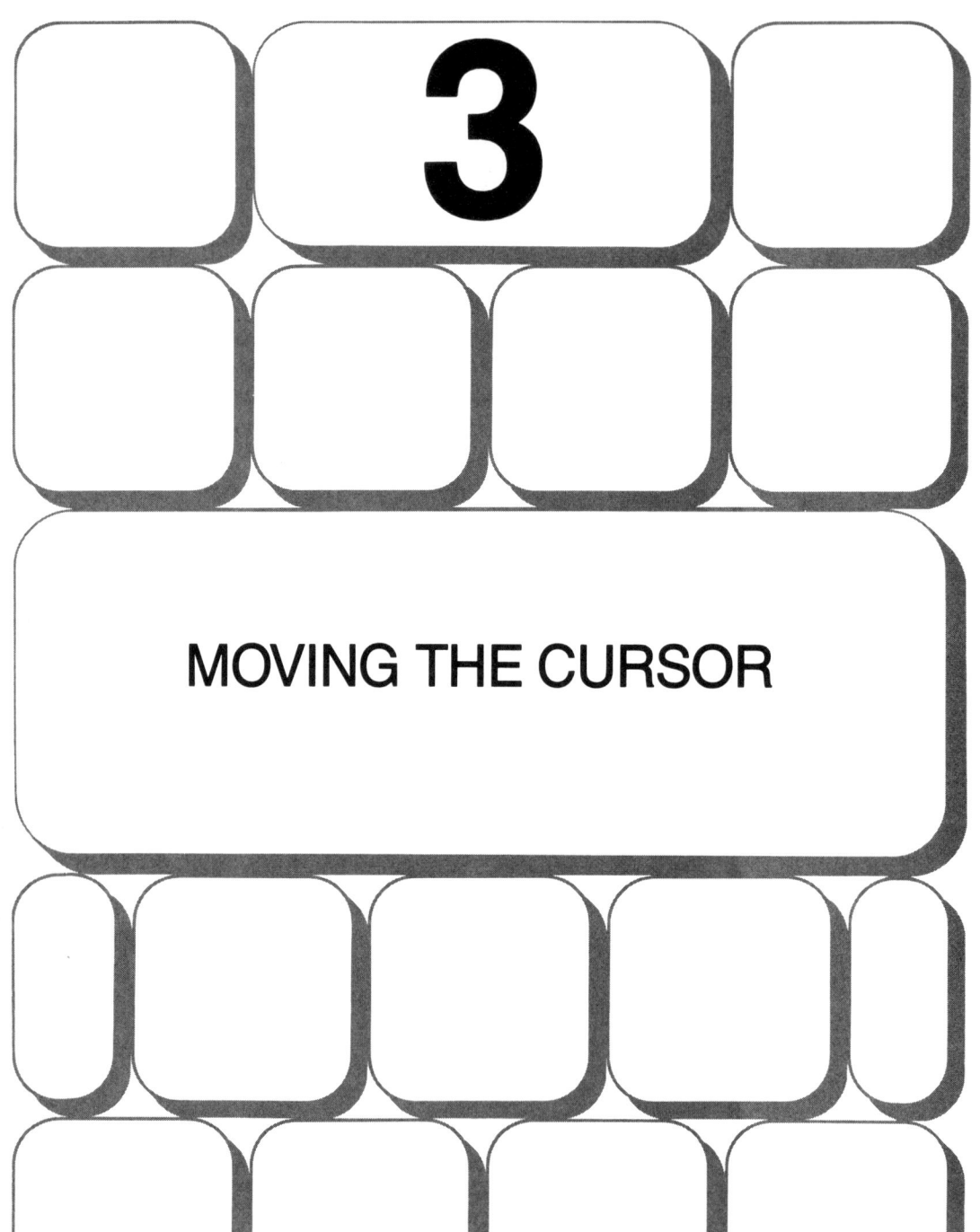

3

MOVING THE CURSOR

In this chapter you will learn new keys that move the cursor quickly from one location to another on the screen and time-saving functions that will quickly position the cursor for the next operation.

There are always several ways to get from one point to another on the screen. Some are quicker or take fewer keystrokes than others, and some are easier to remember. You will probably memorize a few functions quickly and not use the others as often. I would recommend rereading this chapter and Chapter 4 (especially the section on highlighting) after you have used MultiMate for a few weeks to see if you can add a few more functions to your repertoire.

To learn the keys and functions in this chapter, you will need a document at least two screen loads long. If the document named PRACTICE isn't now on the screen, use the *Edit an Old Document* Main Menu choice and follow the screen prompts to get it on the screen. As each key or function is introduced, try it out in the document named PRACTICE.

MOVING TO THE NEXT WORD

You can use any one of the cursor-moving keys to move the cursor under existing characters without affecting them. A cursor-moving key moves the cursor one character at a time and speeds up when you press it continuously.

At times, you will want to move the cursor even faster than this. To move the cursor one word to the right or left without affecting characters it is passing under, hold down Ctrl and press the right cursor mover (→) or the left cursor mover (←).

Note: The cursor will not stop on the first character of a word or group of characters unless that character is a letter or number. This means when the first character is a symbol such as $ or ?, the cursor will jump over it to the next group of characters that does begin with a letter or number. It will also pass over words preceded by screen symbols representing functions such as tab (>>) or center (↔). Finally, *hardspaces* or required spaces (see Chapter 7) will be treated as regular spaces.

Now hold down Ctrl and press the right cursor mover to move the cursor directly to the beginning of the next word to the right.

Repeat the procedure to move rapidly to the beginning of the fourth word in the line.

If you now hold down Ctrl while pressing the left cursor mover, you will move the cursor to the next word to the left. If you repeat the procedure, the cursor will eventually jump all the way to the first word in the line. Once the beginning of a line has been reached, if there is more text, the cursor keeps going to the previous line. After you use Ctrl and the right cursor mover to reach the last word on the right of a line, the cursor will move to the beginning of words in the line below.

MOVING TO THE FIRST OR LAST CHARACTER IN A LINE

To get to the beginning of a line very quickly, press Alt-F3. The cursor will jump directly to the first character in the current line. Now press Alt-F4 to move the cursor directly to the last character in the line.

You might remember these two by thinking of Alt-F3 and Alt-F4 as ALTernate ways of getting to the ends of the line (F3 is on the left; F4 is on the right). Since F3 and F4 are located right next to the tab/backtab key, (⇆), you will be reminded of the left and right ends of the writing line.

You can also use backtab (shift-⇆) to move you to the beginning of your current line. You now have two ways to get quickly to the left edge of the line you are on and one way to get quickly to the right edge of the line you are on.

SCREEN CAPACITY

Before you learn how to move the cursor greater distances, look at what your screen can display.

The first screen of a page will display only 22 lines. The second and subsequent screens of a page don't have a format line at the top, so they will display 23 lines.

Some word processing systems allow you to view an entire page.

MultiMate has been programmed to show 22–23 lines or about one third the number of lines that will fit on an 8½ × 11-inch sheet of paper.

You may find it useful to imagine that the screen is a window. Through it, you view your document as though it had been keyboarded on a continuous sheet of paper like a scroll. The process of viewing the document 22–23 lines at a time is called *scrolling*. Figure 3.1 illustrates how much of your document a screen contains. The square represents the portion you can see.

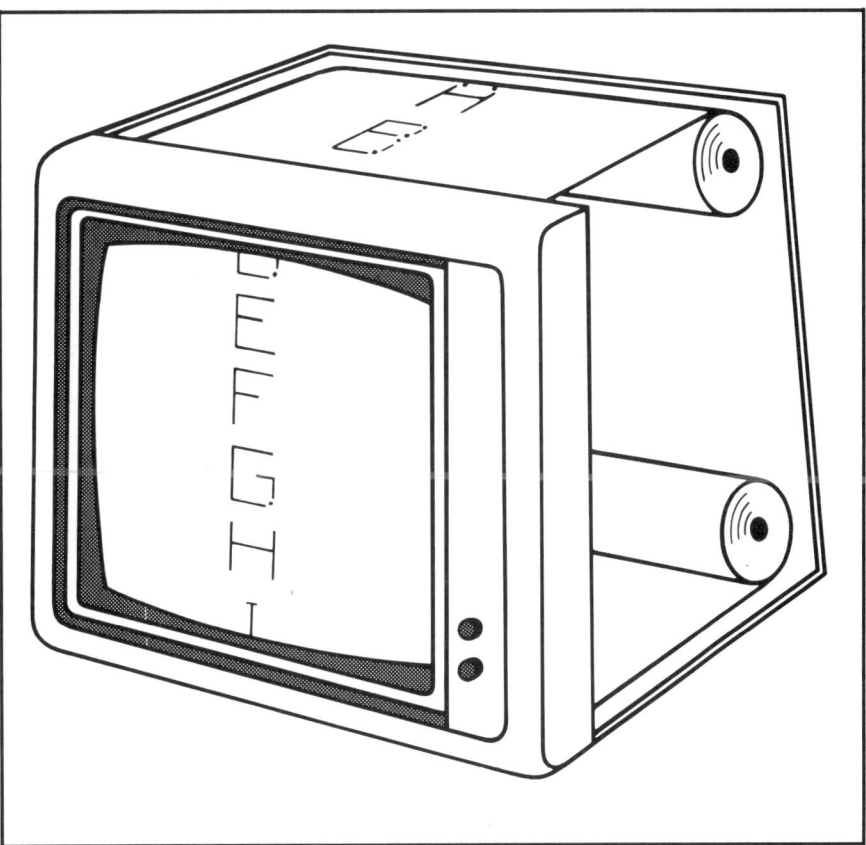

Figure 3.1 – *The portion of a document seen on a MultiMate screen*

GETTING TO THE FIRST OR LAST CHARACTER ON A SCREEN OR PAGE

On a word processor, the first character in the upper left-hand corner of the screen is called the cursor's *home* position. Use the Home key (7 on the numeric keypad) to move the cursor immediately to the first character on the displayed screen. To move the cursor immediately to the first character on the present *page* (rather than the present *screen*) press Ctrl-Home. Of course, if you are on the first screen of a page, these would be the same location.

Press the End key on the numeric keypad to move the cursor immediately to the space following the last character on the present screen. Then use Ctrl-End (the Page End function) to move the cursor to the space following the last character on the page (this may even be one or two screenloads after your present cursor position). Try these four functions now.

MAKING BIGGER JUMPS

The page down key, PgDn, is 3 on the numeric keypad; the page up key, PgUp, is 9 on the numeric keypad. Both of these keys are used to make bigger jumps through a document.

Press PgDn to move the cursor immediately to the nineteenth line below its present position. If there aren't 18 lines left to display, the cursor will jump to the space after the last character on the screen.

Now press the End key to move the cursor to the last character of the page. Then when you press PgDn, the cursor will jump to the first character of the next page, if there is one. If there is no next page, a screen prompt tells you

   THIS IS THE LAST PAGE.

Press PgUp now to display the previous 18 lines of text. If there aren't 18 lines of previous text on this page and your cursor is located somewhere within the page, the cursor will move to the first character on the screen. If your cursor is already on the first character of a page, pressing PgUp will move the cursor directly to the space after the last character on the previous page.

If the cursor is on the first character of a screen, press PgUp to move to the first character of the previous screen.

If you practice these in your document, you will become familiar with each of them. Remember that PgDn displays lines following your present cursor position and PgUp displays previous lines.

You can use PgUp and PgDn to scroll through a document one screen at a time. More efficient ways of getting to a specific page without viewing everything in between are covered later in Chapter 6.

Use F10 to save and exit the document PRACTICE for now; you will need it again in Chapter 4.

Summary of Operations Covered in this Chapter

MOVE CURSOR TO:	PRESS
right one character at a time	→ (right cursor mover)
left one character at a time	← (left cursor mover)
beginning of next word	Ctrl-→ (right cursor mover)
beginning of previous word	Ctrl-← (left cursor mover)
first character of line	Alt-F3 or backtab (shift-⇆)
last character of line	Alt-F4
first character on screen	Home
first character of a page	Ctrl-Home
last character on screen	End
last character of a page	Ctrl-End
nineteenth line above	PgUp
nineteenth line below	PgDn

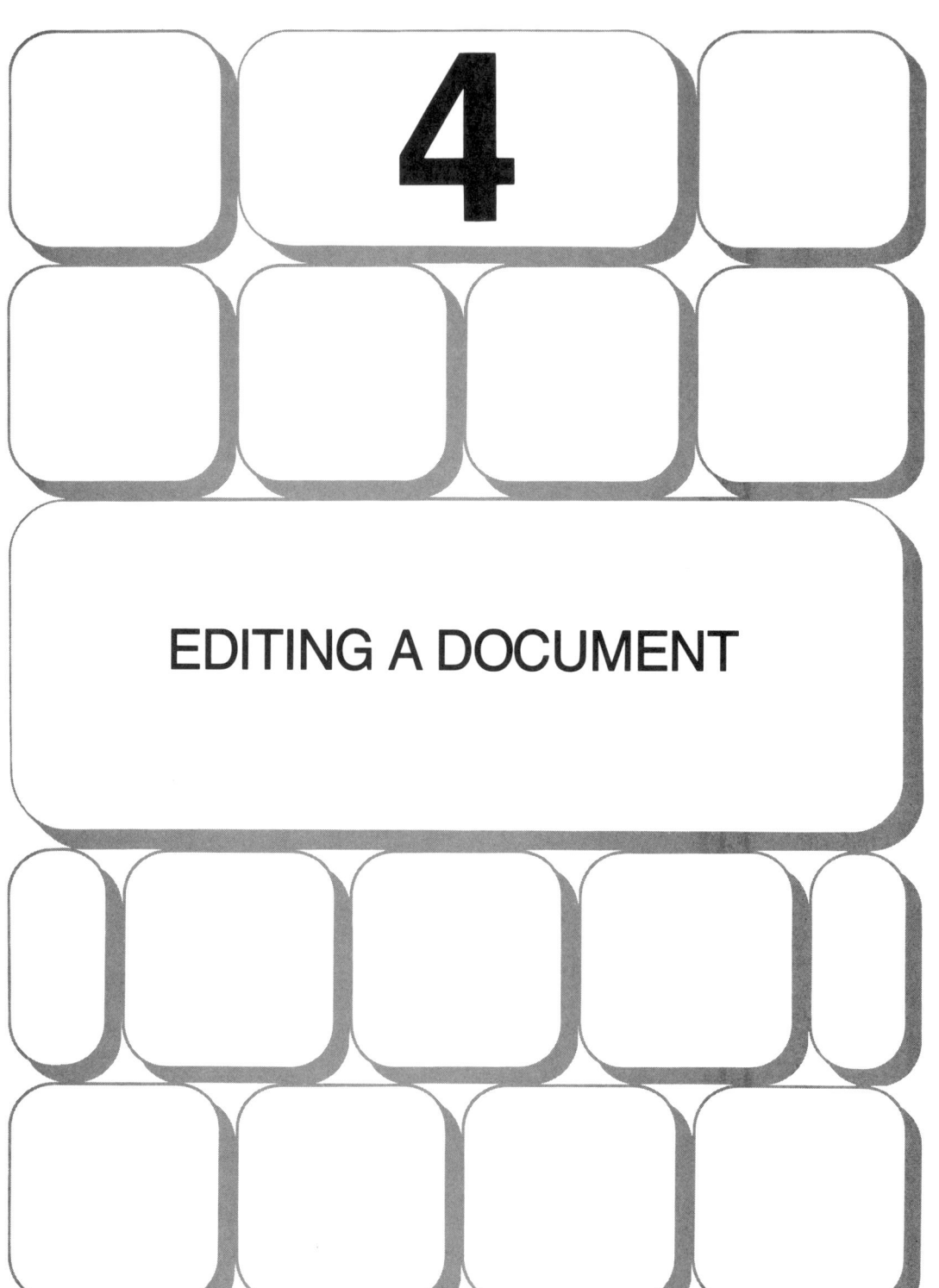

4

EDITING A DOCUMENT

In word processing terminology, *editing* means revising or correcting a document. You can edit as you initially type a document. You can also edit when you call a previously created document to the screen after it has been stored on your disk. You would do this by selecting the first choice you see on the Main Menu: *Edit an Old Document.*

A third type of editing is changing the document defaults after the document has been created. Although it involves editing an old document, this procedure requires a different choice from the Main Menu. It will be covered in Appendix A.

In this chapter you will learn how to do the first two kinds of editing: using strikeover, Insert, and Delete to edit documents as they are being created and then after they are recalled from the document storage disk. More advanced editing functions are covered in Chapters 10 and 11.

STRIKEOVER

Strikeover is used for one-for-one replacement of characters. You can change a character by simply typing another one over it. To replace any character, place the cursor under it, then type the new character over it. If you did this on a piece of paper in a typewriter, you would see one letter on top of the other. On the computer screen, however, the second letter takes the place of the first. Let's try the strikeover method now.

From the Main Menu, press 2 to choose the *Create a New Document* option, and then press return. Name the document EDIT-PRAC and follow the screen prompts to reach the first screen of the document. Fill in the Document Summary Screen as you wish and use the default settings on the Modify Document Defaults Screen.

Type the following sentence exactly as it is shown. *Note:* ≫ means tab and ≪ means return.

≫Word processing will improve your typing speed. ≪

Using the cursor-moving keys, place the cursor under the *t* in *typing.* Now type *productivity* to replace the words *typing speed.* As you type, the new letters replace those that were there.

The corrected sentence should read:

>>Word processing will improve your productivity.<<

Did you notice that when you typed the first *t* of *productivity*, it replaced a blank space between the two words? You replaced one character, the space, with another character, the letter *t*.

It is very important to recognize that spaces, returns, and tabs are characters just as letters are. If your cursor is under one of these when you tap another character, it will be replaced and the arrangement of the text on the screen may be affected.

Here is an example of how the screen will change. Press End to move the cursor to the space after the last character on the screen. Then, type the following text exactly as it is shown:

>>One MultiMate screenload<<
displays 22 or 23 lines of text<<
at a time.<<

With the cursor-moving keys, place the cursor under the return symbol after the word *screenload*. Press the space bar to replace the return symbol (<<) with a space. Repeat this procedure for the return symbol after *text*. Notice that as the returns were replaced by spaces, the text rearranged itself on one line. Just as returns caused subsequent characters to show up on the next line, replacing the return with a space caused those characters to move back to the same line.

If you have followed the directions, the line should now look like this:

>>One MultiMate screenload displays 22 or 23 lines of text at a time.<<

The strikeover method is very effective for correcting simple typographical errors. As you type, you probably tend to hit the correct *number* of letters, but not always the right ones. When you know you have made an error, you can back up and immediately use strikeover to correct it.

INSERTING A SINGLE CHARACTER

Sometimes you need to *add* a space or character where one was omitted, where there are too few characters to make a one-for-one replacement because your new word is longer than the word you are replacing. In either instance you need to use the Single Character Insert function.

Single characters are inserted with the single character insert key, (+), which is located to the far right of the numeric keypad. Place the cursor under the first character (or space) that will *follow* the character you want to insert. Press the single character insert key (+) once to add a space; press the single character insert key again and type a character to add a single character.

Here is an example of Single Character Insert. Press End and type the following, exactly as shown:

>> SouthWestern Oil Company doubled its profit last year. <<

Let's assume the first word is really two words. A space must be inserted between *South* and *Western*.

1. Position the cursor under the *W* of *Western* with the cursor movers.
2. Press the single character insert key (+) to insert a space. (Remember, the key will repeat if held down.)

Now let's add an *s* to *profit*.

1. Place the cursor on the space after *profit*.
2. Press the single character insert key (+) to open up an additional space.
3. Complete the insert by pressing *s*.

To add the *s*, you could also have put the cursor under the space after *profit*, typed an *s*, and then, when the cursor was on the *l* of *last*, pressed + to put back the space between the words. The results would have been the same.

DELETING A SINGLE CHARACTER

To delete a single character, you use the single character delete key (−). It is located at the far right of the numeric keypad above the single character insert key (+).

Now type exactly as shown:

>>Rodger Smythe is the new controller of the company.<<

Then assume you later found out that the fellow's name is really Roger Smyth. To correct this,

1. Place the cursor under the character you want to delete (first the *d* of *Rodger* and then the *e* of *Smythe*).

2. When the cursor is properly positioned press the single character delete key (−) to delete the character.

Be very careful that you don't linger on the single character delete key (−) key; it repeats, and you can easily delete more than you intended. If you accidentally hold it down too long, most computers will sound a beep. If this happens, immediately release the key and wait until there is no activity on the screen. Then go back and insert the characters you didn't mean to delete, using the process described in the next section.

INSERTING MORE THAN ONE CHARACTER

The most efficient way to add more than one consecutive character is to use the insert key (Ins), which is located to the right of the Caps Lock key. Press End and type this example:

>>The president will visit all grand openings of new supermarkets.<<

Since this sentence might be misleading to some readers, let's change it to read *The president of Associated Grocers will visit all grand openings of new supermarkets.*

1. Place the cursor under the *w* of *will*. This is the first character that will follow the inserted material.

2. Press the insert key. The prompt, *INSERT WHAT?* appears in the upper right hand corner of the screen. At the same time, the character above the cursor (and up to 34 characters immediately following it) jumps down to the bottom of the

screen to give you room to type your insert. This line at the bottom of the screen can help you remember when to stop typing characters to be inserted.

As you type the material to be inserted, *of Associated Grocers* (be sure to add a space), it appears *highlighted*, or brighter than the text it follows.

3. To end the insert, press Ins again. Remember, Ins is a toggle key that turns *on* with first tap and *off* with the second. As soon as you press Ins the second time, the 35 characters hop back into place after the material that was inserted, and the screen prompt *INSERT WHAT?* disappears.

CORRECTING WHILE IN INSERT MODE

If you make an error in the material you are inserting, you can move the cursor back to the point of the error and use the strikeover method or the single character insert key (+) or the single character delete key (−) to correct the error. If you then press End, the cursor will move to the end of the material that is being inserted so you can continue.

To correct material other than that which is currently being inserted, you must first get out of Insert mode.

To see how this works, let's insert the name, *John Jones,* after the word *Grocers* in the previous example.

1. First move the cursor to the space after *Grocers.*

2. Press Ins to get into Insert mode.

3. Type a comma, a space, and *John Jones.* All will be highlighted because you are in Insert mode.

4. Before you press Ins to end Insert mode, you suddenly remember that the president's first name is really *Joan.* Move the cursor back to the *h* and replace it with an *a* by using strikeover.

5. Press End to move the cursor into position to continue the insert operation.

6. Finally, type the comma needed after the name and then press Ins to get out of Insert mode.

The corrected sentence should read:

> ≫The President of Associated Grocers, Joan Jones, will visit all grand openings of new supermarkets. ≪

If you are in Insert mode and change your mind about inserting, you can press Esc once to restore the text to its original condition. Try this out to see how it works. (*Note:* sp stands for space.)

1. Move the cursor back to the *J* of *Joan* in the previous sentence. Assume you have decided to put *Mrs.* before Joan's name.
2. Press Ins to get into Insert mode.
3. Type *Mrs.*(sp).
4. Now change your mind about adding this extra word. Press Esc once. You will exit Insert mode and the original sentence will be restored.
   Note: If you accidentally hold Esc down too long, the prompt *Do you wish to escape without saving this page? (Y/N)* will appear. If it does, be sure to answer *N*, or the page you are working on will not be saved to the document-storage disk.

DELETING MORE THAN ONE CHARACTER

Del, also a toggle key, is used to delete more than one character at a time. Let's see how it works by deleting some words from the sentence you were just working with. Let's remove *grand openings of new*.

1. Place the cursor under the first character you want to delete, the *g* of *grand*.
2. Press the delete key, Del, (found just to the right of the space bar and Ins) once, to get into Delete mode. A prompt appears in the upper right hand corner of the screen: *DELETE WHAT?*

You indicate which characters you want to delete by a process called *highlighting*. You can adjust the screen brightness or contrast knobs on your monitor to make highlighted characters even brighter if you need to.

3. Now press the right cursor mover until all words through *new* (sp) are highlighted. (In the next section, you learn how to highlight with several other methods as well.)

Always check to be sure you really do want to delete all the characters that are highlighted. (Once you have pressed Del, it will be too late to retrieve anything that was highlighted!) Once the characters are highlighted, press Del again to complete the function. The words disappear.

When you are in the Delete mode, you *can* change your mind and press Esc to restore things to the way they were before you pressed Del. But remember not to hold Esc down too long!

The sentence should now read:

>>The president of Associated Grocers, Joan Jones, will visit all supermarkets. <<

HIGHLIGHTING METHODS

You have learned to use highlighting with Delete mode. Highlighting is also used for functions which will be covered later: Move, Copy, and External Copy. Because you will use it often, it is important for you to know how to highlight efficiently.

In addition to using the right cursor mover, there are several other ways which rapidly move the cursor to highlight. You will always highlight in response to a prompt such as *DELETE WHAT?*, *MOVE WHAT?*, and *COPY WHAT?*, which means you are always in the midst of the function when you use these techniques. Here is a list of highlighting methods:

TO HIGHLIGHT THIS:	DO THIS:
Everything up to next occurrence of a character	Press any letter, number, or other character to highlight everything up to and including the next occurrence of that character.

Word	a. If the cursor is not on the *first* character of the word, press Alt-F5 to highlight the entire word and the following space. b. If the cursor *is* on the first character of a word, press a space to highlight the entire word.
Line	a. Press Alt-F6 to highlight the entire line the cursor is on from the left edge to the right edge of the screen. The cursor can be located anywhere on the line. b. Press the down cursor mover to highlight from the present cursor position to same position on the next line down. c. Press Alt-F4 to highlight from the present cursor position to the right end of that line.
Sentence	Press Alt-F7 to highlight all text to the left and right up to the next typical end-of-sentence punctuation (., ?, !). The cursor can be located anywhere in the sentence.
Paragraph	a. Press Alt-F8 to highlight all text to the left and to the right of the cursor up to the next return symbol. b. If your cursor is on the *first* character of the paragraph, press return to highlight up to the next return symbol which is typically the end of the paragraph. *Note:* Do not use this technique when a format line is between your present cursor position and

Rest of the screen	the return at the end of a paragraph you are highlighting. Press End to highlight all text from the cursor position up to and including the last character on the screen.
Rest of the page	Press Ctrl-End to highlight all text from the present cursor position up to and including the last character on the current page.
Next page	Press Ctrl-PgDn to highlight all text from the present cursor location to the first character or screen symbol on the next page.
More than one page	Press F1 (the Go To function key), type a page number in the brackets, and then press return to highlight all text up to and including the first character on the page specified.
Rest of the document	Press F1 (the Go To function key), type 999 in the brackets, and press return to highlight through the *first* character of the last page. Then use Ctrl-End to highlight through the last character of the last page.

DEHIGHLIGHTING METHODS

To dehighlight material because you have changed your mind about deleting, moving, or copying it, press the left cursor mover, up cursor mover, backspace, Home (to go to the first highlighted character on a screen) or Ctrl-Home (to go to the first character highlighted on a page).

If you want to abandon an operation completely, press Esc and all highlighted text will automatically dehighlight and be restored to its original condition.

Now try the highlighting and dehighlighting methods just presented. Press End and then type the following paragraphs. Your lines may end in different places than those shown.

>>Producing documents on your computer when it is programmed to act like word processor is different from using a typewriter. The text will first appear on the screen where it can be proofread and edited before it is committed to paper. The paper copy is called a "hard copy." <<
<<
>>Some word processors also allow the operator to enter information directly from the keyboard to the paper in the printer. This is called operating in a "hot print" mode. <<
<<

1. Start with the cursor on the first tab symbol of the first paragraph and get into Delete mode by pressing Del.

2. Type a period to highlight the first sentence, then press the right cursor mover to highlight the next six characters, one at a time.

3. Press the space bar four times to highlight the next four words.

4. Press the down cursor mover twice to highlight the next two lines.

5. Press return twice to highlight the rest of the text.

6. Suppose you now change your mind. Press Esc to get out of Delete mode without deleting anything.

7. Starting with the cursor back on the tab symbol at the beginning of the second paragraph press Del to get into Delete mode and then press return to rapidly highlight the paragraph.

8. Now press Del to delete all of your highlighted text. The first paragraph should still be on the screen.

A COMBINATION OF METHODS

You can also use a combination of strikeover and Insert or Delete methods. For example, do the following to replace the word *text* with the word *document* in the paragraph on the screen.

1. Put your cursor under the first *t* of *text*.
2. Use the strikeover method to replace the four characters of *text* with *docu* and press Ins to get into Insert mode.
3. Now type *ment* to complete the word *document*.
4. Press Ins to toggle out of Insert mode.

Here's another example of using a combination of methods; this time we'll use the same material and replace a long word, *document* with a shorter one, *text*.

1. Put the cursor under the *d* of *document* and use strikeover to type the four new letters of the word *text*.
2. Press Del and highlight *ment*.
3. Press Del again to complete the operation. You could also press the single character delete key (−) four times to get rid of the extra characters of the longer word.

SAVING A DOCUMENT

In Chapter 2, you learned three ways to exit a document. Two of these methods saved your document to disk in the process. There is another way to save your work to disk and still remain in the document.

Press shift-F10 to save the document, including any revisions you have just completed, and the cursor will stay on the document page. (You can remember this by associating the *s* of shift with the *s* of save and stay.) Try it now. You will see the prompt, *PLEASE WAIT* appear briefly on the screen while the document is being stored.

You can use this function to save your changes to a previously stored document which you have recalled and are now editing. It is a good idea to use shift-F10 as a precaution about every 15 minutes while you are working. That way, only the most recent corrections that haven't yet been saved to disk are lost if there is a power failure or some other mishap.

As was explained in Chapter 2, when you are finished creating or editing a document, you can save the document and exit to the Main Menu by pressing F10.

No matter which method you use to save your document, the latest edit of the document replaces what was filed on the disk under that document name. Tap F10 now to save the document and exit to the Main Menu.

RECALLING A DOCUMENT

Now use the Main Menu choice, *Edit an Old Document* (press 1 and return), to recall the document named PRACTICE for editing. Follow the screen prompts until the document is on the screen.

Proofread the document on the screen to find your errors. When you find an error, use strikeover, Single Character Insert, Single Character Delete, Insert, or Delete techniques to correct it.

When you are certain you have corrected all errors, do one of the following:

a. If you want to continue this session at the computer and go on to Chapter 5 now, press shift-F10 to save the corrections you just made to the disk and stay in the document.

b. If you want to stop working on the computer for now, press F10. The corrections you made will be saved to the document storage disk and the Main Menu will be returned to the screen. You can then remove your disks and turn the system off.

SUMMARY OF OPERATIONS COVERED IN THIS CHAPTER

Strikeover

1. Position cursor under the first character to be replaced.
2. Type the new character.

Inserting a Single Character

1. Position the cursor under the first character to follow the inserted character.

2. Press the single character insert key (+) to open up a space.
3. If appropriate, type the character you want to insert.

Deleting a Single Character

1. Position the cursor under the space or character to be deleted.
2. Press the single character delete key (−) to delete the character above the cursor.

Inserting More Than One Character

1. Position the cursor under the first character to follow the inserted material.
2. Press Ins to get into Insert mode.
3. Type the characters to be inserted.
4. Press Ins to get out of Insert mode.

Deleting More Than One Character

1. Position the cursor under the first character to be deleted.
2. Press Del to get into Delete mode.
3. Highlight the characters you want deleted.
4. Press Del again to exit Delete mode.

5

FORMATTING A DOCUMENT

The term *format* refers to the arrangement of text on a document page. A document's format includes such things as line spacing (e.g., single, double, triple, etc.), tab settings, and writing line length.

A COMPARISON OF TYPEWRITER FORMATTING WITH MULTIMATE FORMATTING

On a typewriter, you set a tab stop by spacing to the point where you want the tab set and then pressing a key or lever. The margins, which determine the number of horizontal spaces in the writing line, are usually set with a key, a lever, or sliding stops. Pitch, the number of characters printed per horizontal inch (usually 10 or 12, i.e. pica or elite) may also be set on more sophisticated typewriters. Vertical spacing is set with the line space regulator lever.

With MultiMate, you set tab stops, writing line length, and vertical line spacing in the format line; you set the left margin and pitch when you print.

The main difference between the two is that you have more flexibility with MultiMate. You can experiment or, if you change your mind, you can reformat and print again. On a typewriter, you would have to retype the whole document to try out different formats.

THINKING IN TERMS OF SPACES IN THE WRITING LINE

A writing line on the screen begins at column 0 and may extend up to column 156 (even though you couldn't see all of it on the screen at once). When you print, you determine the left margin or point at which the writing line will begin printing. You do not set a right margin; the system automatically determines the right margin by adding the writing line length to the left margin you set when you print.

Here's how to figure the number of spaces you would want to set in the writing line to have one inch side margins. Assume the pitch will be set at 10 characters per inch (pica) when you print, and assume the paper is a standard 8^1/$_2$ inches wide (85 pica characters). A one-inch (10 space) left margin and one-inch (10 space) right margin equals a total of 20 spaces in margins. So, 85 available spaces on the paper minus 20 spaces in margins leaves 65 spaces to put in the writing line.

Here's how to figure the length of the writing line if you are going to use an elite (12 characters per inch) pitch setting, standard paper, and one-inch side margins. The total spaces available on the paper (8½ inches times 12 characters per inch) is 102 spaces. The total spaces in two one-inch side margins is 24 spaces. 102 minus 24 gives you a writing line length of 78 spaces.

THE LIMITS OF THE SCREEN DISPLAY

The maximum width of the writing line is 156 characters. The screen, however, displays a maximum of 80 characters. If you choose to have a writing line that is wider than 80 characters, one end of the line won't show up on the screen.

To view the portion of the writing line that is not visible on screen, move the cursor toward that side of the screen with the cursor-moving keys. Note that when the right edge of the line comes into view, the left edge disappears temporarily. (The reverse is also true.) Moving left or right to view the entire writing line is called *horizontal scrolling*.

GENERAL INFORMATION ABOUT FORMAT LINES

Here is some additional information to help you understand MultiMate format lines. We will then look at how to change them to tailor the arrangement of a document to fit your needs.

The main point to remember about a format line is that it controls all text below it. When a document contains several format lines, each will affect only the text directly below it.

A new format line can be placed anywhere in a document, and it will remain in effect until another format line is encountered. These format lines are permanently stored with the document and don't have to be recreated each time the document is recalled.

The format lines you see on the screen are different from text in a couple of ways. First, although they appear on the screen, format lines are not counted in the status line line-count figure. Format lines also differ from text in that they are not printed with the text when you use the MultiMate Print utility. They would be printed if you used the Print Screen command, because it commits every symbol and character on the screen to paper. The Print Screen command is discussed in Chapter 9.

Although text always appears single spaced on the screen, it will be printed with whatever spacing is set in the format line.

The following numbers are used in column two of the format line to indicate the line spacing with which you want the document printed:

    0 zero spacing (overstrike)   = two and one-half spacing
    1 single spacing (default setting)   + one and one-half spacing
    2 double spacing   H half spacing
    3 triple spacing   Q quarter spacing

You can set formats either before or after typing a document. You can even type text using one format line and then add a different format line. The text automatically changes to reflect the characteristics of the new format line.

All format operations use F9, the Format Change key. F9 is a toggle key and is sometimes used with various other keys.

THE SYSTEM DEFAULT FORMAT LINE

As described in Chapter 2, MultiMate documents have a preset or system default format line which appears on the second line of the first screen of every new page you create.

If the system default format line's line spacing, tab settings, and writing line length are not those you most commonly use, you can permanently change them. You will see how to do this Appendix A, Other Utilities.

INSERTING FORMAT LINES WITHIN A DOCUMENT

You can insert any of three types of format lines wherever you wish in your document. You might do this just to review a format line, but usually you insert it to modify text. Here are the options you have:

1. Press Ctrl-F9 to insert a copy of the system default format line. The prompt, *FORMAT SYSTEM,* displays until you toggle out of Format mode.
2. Press Alt-F9 to insert a copy of the format line that is at the top of the page you are currently on. *FORMAT PAGE* appears as a prompt.
3. Press shift-F9 to insert a copy of the format line currently in effect (although possibly not shown on this screen). The prompt, *FORMAT CURRENT* displays.

The format line is inserted on the screen on the line above your present cursor postion, and a prompt will appear at the upper right of the screen to tell you what type of format line you are inserting. The cursor appears in the format line so you could modify it or abort the operation. Finally you must press F9 to toggle out of Format mode and return your cursor to its previous location.

MODIFYING A FORMAT LINE

Any format line can be modified. *Note:* In order to modify it, the cursor must be located in the format line. If you have just inserted a format line, the cursor will already be in it. If the format line is already displayed, position the cursor on any character below it and press F9.

F9 is a toggle key you use for all Format Change operations. Press it once to get into Format mode. This causes the prompt *FORMAT CHANGE* to display, and puts the cursor into the format line. Pressing it a second time puts any changes you've made into effect and takes you out of Format Change mode.

If you change your mind while the cursor is still in the format line, you can restore everything to its original condition by pressing Esc.

Let's try some of these functions. If the document PRACTICE is not currently on your screen, choose *Edit an Old Document* from the Main Menu. Follow the screen prompts to get to the first page of the document. We will start with the cursor below the system default format line that is in effect.

1. Press F9, the Format Change key. A prompt in the upper right-hand corner of the screen says *FORMAT CHANGE*. The cursor hops into the format line at column 3. (The status line has a column indicator at the right end.)
2. Backspace once so the cursor is under the number 1 (the default setting for single line-spacing) in column 2.
3. Type 2 over the 1 to change the line spacing to double spacing.

Now change all the tab settings.

1. Press the space bar to move the cursor to column 6. Spacing under the tab symbol (>>) at column 5 made it disappear.
2. Next, use right cursor mover to move the cursor to the tab symbol at column 15. Notice that using the cursor-moving key did not affect the tab at column 10.
3. Use the space bar to delete the tab at column 15.
4. Then with either the space bar or the right cursor mover, move the cursor to column 30.
5. Press tab to set a new tab stop at column 30. A tab symbol (>>) will appear.

Finally, to set the new writing line length,

6. Move the cursor to column 60 with the space bar or with the right cursor mover.
7. When the cursor is at 60, press return to put a return symbol (<<) there. The writing line length is now set at 60 spaces.
8. Press F9 to exit Format Change mode and put the new format settings into effect. The cursor automatically returns to the character under which it was located before you pressed F9.

Notice that the text below the new format line automatically conforms to the new format immediately. Unlike other word processing programs, MultiMate does not require you to perform a separate step to align the text after changing format settings.

CREATING AN ALTERNATE FORMAT LINE WITHIN A DOCUMENT

Sometimes you want to have sections of a document formatted differently. For example, in a double-spaced document, there might be a lengthy quote or legal property description that you want to single space with indented margins. You would format this section of your document with an alternate format line.

To see how an alternate format line is created within a document, let's reformat the second paragraph of PRACTICE so it will have single spacing, a tab at column 5, and a 40-space writing line.

1. Position the cursor on the first character of the the second paragraph, the *P* of POSITIVE.

2. Press Alt-F9 to get into Format Page mode. A copy of the format line at the top of this page will appear just above the cursor.

3. Backspace once to move the cursor to column 2 and type 1 to set the line spacing to single spacing.

4. Use the right cursor mover to move the cursor to column 40; press return to set a 40-space writing line. (Don't use the space bar to move the cursor or you'll delete your tabs!)

5. Press F9 to exit Format Page mode. The text below the new format line will immediately conform to the new format settings. (Remember, vertical spacing always displays as single spacing.)

6. Because we want only the second paragraph to be formatted differently, we need to insert another format line for paragraphs after the second. Move the cursor to a character in the first line of the third paragraph.

7. Insert a copy of the format line currently displayed at the top of the page by pressing Alt-F9. This will restore the original format to paragraph 3 and later paragraphs.
8. Press F9 to exit Format Page mode and put the changes into effect.

DELETING A FORMAT LINE

You might want to delete a format line because you have decided you don't want to change the format after all. You do this by using Del.

Place the cursor under a character below the format line you want to delete. If for some reason there is none, you could type one and delete it later if necessary. Let's delete some format lines now.

1. In the document that is still on the screen, use the cursor-moving keys to position the cursor anywhere on the screen under the third format line.
2. Press Del. The prompt *DELETE WHAT?* appears in the upper right-hand corner of the screen.
3. Press F9, the Format Change key, to indicate that you want to delete a format line.
4. Press Del again to exit Delete mode. The format line disappears from the page, and the text conforms to the format line above it.
5. Repeat the process to delete all format lines except the one at the top of the page.
6. Press F10 to save and exit the document and return to the Main Menu.

Note: The format line at the top of a page and a return immediately preceding any format line cannot be deleted.

SUMMARY OF OPERATIONS COVERED IN THIS CHAPTER

Inserting Format Lines into a Document

1. Position the cursor on the line that will follow the inserted format line.
2. Press Ctrl-F9, Alt-F9, or shift-F9 depending on which kind of format line you want to insert) to display the format line and move the cursor into it.
3. Make any desired changes.
4. Press F9 to exit Format mode and put the changes into effect.

Modifying a Format Line

1. Place the cursor on any character under the format line you want to change.
2. Press F9 to get into Format mode and move the cursor into the format line.
3. Make your changes (see below).
4. Press F9 to exit Format mode and put changes into effect.

Making Changes in a Format Line

1. Start with the cursor in the format line (see above).
2. Change line spacing by backspacing to move the cursor into column 2 and typing over the number which is there.
3. Change tabs by moving the cursor (with the cursor- moving keys or space bar) to the appropriate column and pressing tab.
4. Set writing line length by moving the cursor to the correct column and pressing return.

Deleting a Format Line

1. Position the cursor on a character below the format line you want to delete.
2. Press Del to get into Delete mode; the prompt *DELETE WHAT?* appears.
3. Press F9 to indicate you want the format line deleted.
4. Press Del to exit Delete mode.

6
ADVANCED FORMATTING FUNCTIONS

A MultiMate document consisting of more than one page contains a page break. This chapter will explain how that page break got into your document and also how to move the cursor rapidly through a multipage document.

AUTOMATIC PAGE BREAKS

A page break (i.e. new page) will be *automatically* created for you if you have specified Y after *Automatic Page Breaks?* on the Modify Document Defaults Screen. This is a new feature of the 3.2 update version. Unless you change it, each page will be 55 lines long because that is the default or preset number of lines per page.

If you specify N after *Automatic Page Breaks?* on the Modify Document Defaults Screen, the system merely reminds you to create a new page by lighting up the *LINE* number spot in the status line when you reach line 55. You then may continue to type up to the maximum number of lines a MultiMate page may contain (150). The system does nothing more than alert you with the lighted line number and a possible beep because you have indicated you don't want automatic page breaks inserted for you.

You would need to type in a document that is longer than 56 lines to be able to try out the automatic page break function. Rather than do that now, just notice in your next long document when the system automatically creates a new page for you. You will know this is happening because *PLEASE WAIT* appears on the screen as you type line 55. Then the cursor reappears on a screen which displays only a status line (indicating *PAGE: 2*) and a new format line.

CHANGING THE NUMBER OF LINES PER PAGE

You have two opportunities to change the number of lines contained on each page. First, you can change this number on the Modify Document Defaults Screen (which appears right after the Document Summary Screen) after the *Number of Lines Per Page?* prompt.

Second, if you want to change the number after you have already started typing the document, press Alt-F2. This screen prompt displays: *PAGE LINE LENGTH? [55]*. Type the new number of lines per page over the *55* and press return or F10 to set the new page length.

If you are using standard size typing paper that is 8½ by 11 inches, it could contain 66 lines of type if every single line on the sheet were used. Since you usually want to have a top and bottom margin each of at least an inch (6 lines), you would leave a total of 12 lines blank. Subtract the 12 lines of the top and bottom margins from 66 total lines available. This leaves 54 lines for the typed text. The authors of MultiMate chose to have 55 lines typed on by default.

We'll try this function in combination with others later in this chapter.

MANUALLY CREATING NEW PAGES

You manually create a new page by using the Page Break function key (F2); no graphic symbol is placed on the screen. The page break occurs *before* the present cursor position. This means that the character the cursor is under when you press F2 will be the first one on the new page. So, if you are beginning a new page with a new indented paragraph, place the cursor under the tab graphic, not under the first letter of the first word.

Note: The format line at the *top* of a page will be duplicated at the top of the next page (i.e. after a page break). This is true even if another format line is in effect part way down the first page.

If your printer spews out blank sheets of paper, you may have held F2, the Page Break key, down too long and created more pages than you intended. Since the cursor waits on the last page created for you to begin typing, you may not have noticed that you unintentionally created blank pages between pages of text.

Let's manually create new page breaks in the document, PRACTICE. Choose *Edit an Old Document* from the Main Menu and follow screen prompts to recall PRACTICE to the screen.

After the format changes you made in Chapter 5, PRACTICE should now have a 60 space writing line and double spacing. It was created without automatic page breaks so it should be a one-page document of about 106 lines.

You will use manual page breaks to make this a three page document which has only two or three paragraphs on each page. Remember to release F2 very quickly or you may end up with extra blank pages.

Place the cursor under the first character of paragraph three, the E of *Efficient*. Press F2. Note that after the *PLEASE WAIT* prompt disappears, your cursor is on page 2.

Move the cursor to the G of *General* and repeat the process to create page 3.

DELETING PAGE BREAKS TO COMBINE PAGES

To combine two pages, delete the page break between them. Place the cursor on the last character of the first page (press Ctrl-End to get there) and press shift-F2. Try this now by pressing PgUp until the cursor is on page 1 and then pressing Ctrl-End to place the cursor on the last character of the page. Press shift-F2 to remove the page break to combine page 1 and page 2 into a single page containing about 64 lines. When combining two pages, the cursor must be placed at the end of the first of the two pages before shift-F2 is pressed.

Caution: MultiMate pages can have a maximum of 150 lines. Do not combine pages if doing so will put more than 150 lines on a single page; if you do, you may lose some of your document.

AUTOMATICALLY REPAGINATING A DOCUMENT

You can automatically reestablish page breaks throughout your whole document with a specified number of lines on each page.

The common word processing term for this is *global pagination*. *Global* refers to a function that takes place through an entire document. Global pagination is usually performed *after* the entire document is keyboarded; but because MultiMate pages must not exceed

150 lines, put in temporary page breaks in a document that is longer than 2½ pages.

To repaginate PRACTICE globally, press PgUp until the cursor is under the first character of the document (or other point at which you want repagination to begin). Then, press Ctrl-F2. The screen prompt indicates you are in *REPAGINATION MODE,* and you are asked to *Enter Lines Per Page: [ ].* Enter the number of lines you want on a page and press return. For our purposes, enter 36 and press return. A screen prompt indicates *Repaginating—PLEASE WAIT,* and the system automatically deletes existing page breaks and inserts the new page breaks with the specified number of lines on each page.

If you entered N when asked asked about *widows and orphans* on the Modify Document Defaults Screen, the system won't leave one line of a paragraph at the bottom of a page or carry over only one line of a paragraph to a new page when it repaginates.

PRACTICE is now three pages long. Leave it on the screen for later use.

REQUIRED PAGE BREAKS

If you want to have a page break always occur at a specific spot, you can create a *required page break.* This means that during automatic repagination, the line count you gave would be ignored, and the required page break would stand.

A regular page break is made with F2. To create a required page break, place the cursor under the first character of the new page and press Alt-B (lower- or uppercase). When you do so, a *PLEASE WAIT* prompt displays, the required page break symbol (⊥) appears where the cursor was, and the cursor moves to the top of the next page.

You can use a required page break when you have a table or illustration that must remain intact on one page. You could also end a page even though it's only half full so a major new section of a long report will begin at the top of a new page.

DELETING REQUIRED PAGE BREAKS

Regular page breaks are removed when a document is repaginated and they are no longer needed at a location because of the new line count.

However, required page breaks are deleted only when you put the cursor on the required page break symbol(⊥) and the single character delete key (−) once or Del twice.

Although there was no need to put required page breaks in PRACTICE, you could try creating and deleting a required page break now if you wish. Be sure to repaginate after you have deleted the required page break.

MOVING THROUGH PAGES

In Chapter 3 you learned some ways to move the cursor rapidly. You will now learn additional ways to move the cursor rapidly through a longer document.

Ctrl-PgUp will take you to the end of the previous page, and Ctrl-PgDn will take you to the beginning of the following page. Use Ctrl-PgUp now to move the cursor to the first character of PRACTICE.

If you want to move either forward or backward quickly across more than one page, use the Go To key. Press F1 now and the screen prompt asks *GO TO PAGE? [ ]*. Type 3, the number of the page you want to go to, and press return. Your cursor will move rapidly to the first character of page 3.

You can also use F1 to specify options other than specific page numbers. When the screen prompt asks *GO TO PAGE? [ ]*, you can use the following combinations to move the cursor to the first character of the first or last page:

F1, 1, then return, or F1, Home	first character of first page
F1, 999, then return, or F1, End	first character of last page

Press F1 Home now to move the cursor to the first character of the first page. Then press F1-End to move the cursor to the first character of page 3.

USING THE PLACE MARK FUNCTION

You can also use F1 to set a *place marker*. With the Place Mark function, you mark characters so you can rapidly return to them. For example, you might mark your place so you can return to it after editing another section. You could also use a place marker to pick up where you left off the day before or mark a word whose spelling you need to check or for which you want to choose a synonym.

Let's set the place marker now, under the first character of page 3. Since the cursor is already under the character you wish to mark, press Alt-F1. You can tell a place marker has been set because the marked character will be flashing. Then press F1-Home.

When you are ready to advance to a place marker, be sure the cursor is at any location before the place marker, as it is now. Then press Ctrl-F1. The cursor will move to the next flashing character immediately.

You can remove a place marker by reversing the process you used to set it. That is, put the cursor under the flashing character and press Alt-F1. You can also just type over the flashing character with the same character. Use strikeover to replace the flashing character and thus remove the place mark. Press F10 to save and exit the document.

SUMMARY OF OPERATIONS COVERED IN THIS CHAPTER

Changing the Number of Lines per Page
Prior to Starting the Document

1. From the Main Menu, choose *Create a New Document* and press return.

2. Name the document and press F10 to access the Modify Document Defaults screen.

3. Change the number after the *Number of Lines per Page* line.
4. Press F10.

Changing the Number of Lines per Page from within the Document

1. Press Alt-F2
2. Indicate the number of lines per page after the *PAGE LINE LENGTH? [ ]* prompt appears.

Manually Creating New Pages

1. Place the cursor under the character you want to be first on the new page.
2. Press F2.

Deleting Page Breaks to Combine Pages

1. Place the cursor on the last character of the first of the two pages that are to be combined.
2. Press shift-F2.

Automatically Repaginating a Document

1. Place the cursor on the first character of the portion to be repaginated.
2. Press Ctrl-F2.
3. Enter the number of lines per page after the prompt.
4. Press return and repagination begins.

Required Page Breaks

1. Place the cursor on the first character to be on the new page.
2. Press Alt-B.

Deleting a Required Page Break

1. Place the cursor under the required page break symbol.
2. Press the Single Character Delete key (−) once or Del twice.

Setting a Place Marker

1. Place the cursor on the character to be marked.
2. Press Alt-F1.
3. The place-marked character will continue flashing until the place marker is removed.

Removing a Place Marker

1. Place the cursor on the flashing character.
2. Press Alt-F1 or retype the character.
3. Character will stop flashing.

Moving through a Document

to end of previous page	Ctrl-PgUp
to beginning of following page	Ctrl-PgDn
to first character of first page	F1 Home
to first character of specified page	F1 (page #) return
to first character of last page	F1 (999) return or F1 End
to Place Marker	Ctrl-F1

7

SPECIAL FEATURES

In this chapter you will learn about special MultiMate functions that make your life as a typist easier. Create a new document called FEATURES so you will be able to try them as you go through the chapter. Follow the screen prompts to get to the first screen of the document. *Note:* Don't change any document defaults or format settings at this time.

CENTER

The Center function horizontally centers characters between the ends of the writing line. It is useful for such items as titles of reports or main and secondary headings of tables.

To center text with MultiMate, you merely give the Center instruction when the cursor is at the left edge of the writing line, and then type the line you want centered.

To center the words "SPECIAL FEATURES" in your new document, press F3 to activate the Center function. This will put the center graphic, ↔ , at the center of the writing line. Then type *SPECIAL FEATURES* and tap return to end the Center function.

You can perform editing functions such as strikeover, Delete, and Insert on a centered line. The line will be centered as long as ↔ remains in front of it. Try this example. Move the cursor to the *F* of *FEATURES* and press Ins. Type the word *MULTIMATE* and a space before *FEATURES*. Press Ins again. The line remains centered even though you added another word to it.

Now let's see how to center a line after it has been typed. Tap End to get to the next blank space at the left edge of the writing line. Type the words *CENTER FUNCTION* and press return. We can center this line if we now insert a center graphic (↔) in front of the line. Put the cursor on the *C* of *CENTER*, press the + key, and then press F3. The ↔ appears, and the line of text hops to the center of the writing line.

If you want to have a centered line transformed into regular text, delete the center graphic with the single character delete key (−). The line will then begin at the left margin. To try this out, put the cursor under the ↔ graphic before the word *SPECIAL,* and press the single character delete key. The line moves to the left margin when the ↔ is gone. Center the line once more by putting the cursor on the *S* of *SPECIAL* and pressing first the single character insert key (+) and then F3.

Even if you change format settings such as writing line length, the line will remain centered. Now try this: tap F9 to hop the cursor into the format line, change it to a 50-space writing line length, and tap F9 to exit the format line. Notice that the lines remain centered between the ends of the writing line, even though the length of the writing line changed.

INDENT

Use the Indent function when two or more consecutive lines need to be indented to the same point. This is a temporary left margin which you can use for paragraphs you want indented within a document. Indent is also used for items in a numbered list.

Look at the example of an indented paragraph in Figure 7.1.

The *x* lines represent regular paragraphs indented from the left with a tab and typed with wraparound. The *y* lines represent a paragraph that is indented from the left margin with the Indent function. Notice that an alternate format line was inserted before the indented text. This created a shorter writing line, so wraparound was also in effect for the *y* lines.

When you tab or indent, you must have set tabs in the format line. The difference is that tab is in effect for only one line, and indent is in effect until you press return. Because a return cancels Indent, wraparound must be used in a paragraph featuring Indent.

Try an example using the new 50-space format line you created for the last example. Press End to move the cursor to the end of existing text and press return three times. Type the following paragraph using tab before the first word.

>>This is a very popular sentence for typists
to type rapidly: <<
<<

Now press Alt-F9 to insert an alternate format line. Modify it so it will have only one tab set at position 10 and a writing line of 40 spaces. Press F9 to exit Format mode.

Press F4 to activate the Indent function. The symbol that appears on the screen is →. Now type the following sentence using wrap-around to return at line ends.

→ Now is the time for all good
men and women to come to the
aid of their country. <<

Now insert the current format line from the top of the page by pressing Alt-F9. It has a 50-space writing line and a tab at columns 5, 10, and 15. After you press F9 to move the cursor out of the format line, type the sentence below pressing tab before the first word.

>>Typing it five times is a good way to get
your fingers warmed up before you begin your
typing work for the day. <<

```
|1...>>....>>....>>....................<<    (original format line)
      >>xxx xxxx xxxxx xxxxxxxxx xxxx xx
xxx xxxxxxxxxxxx xxxxx xxxxx xxxx.    <<
|1......>>....................<<             (alternate shortened format line)
        -->yyy yyyyyyyyy yyyyy yyy           (wraparound in effect at line ends)
           yyy yyyyyyy yyyyy yyy
           yyyyy yyy yyyyyyy yyy.  <<
|1...>>....>>....>>....................<<    (original format line restored)
      >>xx xxxxxx xxxxxxxxx xxxxx xxxx x
xxxxx xxxxxxx x xxxxxxx xxx xxxx.   <<
```

Figure 7.1 – *An indented paragraph.*

The first and last paragraphs should have only the first line indented, and the middle paragraph should have all lines indented as shown below.

>>This is a very popular sentence for typists
to type rapidly: <<
<<
→ Now is the time for all good
men and women to come to the
aid of their country. <<
>>Typing it five times is a good way to get
your fingers warmed up before you begin your
typing work for the day. <<

DECIMAL TABS

Another special MultiMate function which uses a tab stop set in the format line is Decimal Tab, represented by ▌ on the screen. Decimal Tab (known as Dec Tab for short) aligns columns of numbers around a decimal point or right justifies, as shown below:

▌ 8364.513   ▌ 42.651   ▌ 8600<<
   ▌ 1.1   ▌ .1244   ▌ End<<
<<

Notice that the decimals in the numbers in the first two columns are lined up under one another. The third column shows two other uses of Dec Tab:

a. For whole numbers: if there is no decimal point in a number, the system aligns it after the last number.
b. For words: Dec Tab doesn't distinguish betweeen alpha characters and numeric characters. It also aligns words after the last character.

Try the Dec Tab function by reproducing the table above on your screen. First press Alt-F9 to create an alternate format line. Erase the current tabs by spacing under them and set new ones at 16, 27, and 41. Get out of the format line by pressing F9.

Now press shift-F4, for Dec Tab, and the cursor moves to 16, the column at which the first tab stop is set. Then, as you type *8364* of the first number, the characters shift to the left of the tab stop until you type the decimal point. The rest of the number, *513,* moves to the right of the decimal point. Press shift-F4 to move to the next column and type the rest of the example.

MultiMate, an internationally popular program, allows a comma to be used for alignment as well (European style). You must specify decimal point or comma on the Modify Document Defaults screen which appears when you create a new document.

HARDSPACES (REQUIRED SPACES)

As you now know, wraparound automatically moves a word to the next line when it won't fit within the number of spaces set in the format line. In this process, the system sometimes violates typing rules for separating items on two lines. You can prevent items from being separated incorrectly by using a *hardspace* or required space instead of the regular space created by the space bar.

When you press Alt-S, you create a hardspace, which is indicated by the screen symbol ϕ. This screen symbol is for your information only. It will be replaced with a regular space when the document is printed.

Below are examples of items you would want printed on one line rather than word wrapped and printed on two lines. The ϕ's represent hard spaces.

Lynnwood, ϕ WA ϕ 98037	(between city and state; and state and zip)
Leanna ϕ M. Holcomb	(between first name and middle initial)
Mr. ϕ Jack Berglund	(between title and first name)
Y. ϕ M. ϕ C. ϕ A.	(between parts of an abbreviation)

The most efficient way to use a hardspace is to type it as you initially type a document. This will ensure that the words will be divided correctly in all drafts of the document, even if editing changes their positions later. It's easier just to put them in the first place.

Remember, a hardspace doesn't *prevent* wraparound; it only keeps a group of characters together by word wrapping them all to the second line.

Try this example. Tap Alt-F9 to insert the format line from the top of the page (because it has a tab at column 5 that we need). Press F9 to exit Format mode. Type the following sentences beginning with a tab:

>>Ten candidates were interviewed on November 21, 1984. The people who are most likely to be invited back for a second interview on February 11, l985 are Tanya Nelson, Susan M. Simons, G. O. Oertli, and Richard Patterson. <<
<<

Some of the dates and names in this example are separated in undesirable places. Using Alt-S, go back and replace regular spaces with hardspaces after November, February, and Susan, you may have to use PgDn to bring all of the paragraph to the screen. You would usually place hardspaces between the day of the month and the year and between the middle initials and the last names as well. But since this writing line is so short and since there are so many names together, it is better to let the names wrap around after the middle initials.

Tap End to prepare for the next exercise.

SOFT HYPHENS AND HARD HYPHENS

If you type a hyphen in a word, it will always appear in the printed document no matter where that word occurs in the writing line. This required hyphen is referred to as a *hard hyphen.*

But sometimes you will want a *soft hyphen,* printed *only* when the word needs to be divided at the end of a line. If you discover your document has an uneven right margin because long, multisyllabic words have wrapped around, you can use soft hyphens to divide them between two lines.

To create soft hyphens, place the cursor under the first character you want to appear on the next line and press shift-F7. *Note:* If you try to insert a soft hyphen at a point which would put more characters than can fit onto the previous line, your command will be ignored.

The screen graphic ≈ , which appears when you create a soft hyphen, will be replaced with a regular hyphen when the document is printed. If a later rearrangement of the lines puts the word with the soft hyphen in the middle of a line, the soft hyphen will be deleted.

Now try creating a soft hyphen. Using the format line on the screen, type the following lines beginning at the left margin:

>>A computer can be a very useful information
handling and processing tool that is worth its
weight in gold because of the increased
productivity and timesaving which it makes
possible. <<
<<

Notice that the right margin is very uneven because the long words at the right ends of the lines were wrapped around. To even out the writing line, place the cursor on the *l* of *handling* (the first character you want to move to the second line down.) Press shift-F7 to divide the word with a soft hyphen.

On the screen, the soft hyphen looks like this: ≈ , but in the printed document the screen graphic is changed to a regular hyphen.

Let's see what happens to the soft hyphen when the writing line length is changed. Place the cursor on the first line of the paragraph and press Alt-F9 to create an alternate format line. Change the writing line to 60 spaces and tap F9 to exit Format mode. Notice that the soft hyphen is gone because the word in which it was used is no longer wrapped to the beginning of the next line so no longer needs to be divided. If, however, the writing line length were returned to the previous length, the soft hyphen would not come back. Press End and return.

AUTO UNDERLINE-TEXT AND DEUNDERLINE

With MultiMate you can *manually* underline words after you type them by placing the cursor on the first character to be underlined, pressing shift and tapping the hyphen/underline key located left of the backspace.

You can also *automatically* underline words as you type them. Hold Alt and press the hyphen/underline key to put you in Auto Underline-Text mode. On some monitors, a line will display under the S↓N↓ characters in the lower right hand corner of the screen to indicate you are currently in Auto Underline-Text mode. On other monitors, the S↓N↓ and all underlined characters will display in reverse video (the background is light colored and the character is dark).

Try using Auto Underline-Text mode now. Press Alt and the hyphen/underline key, then type the following sentence using Caps Lock as needed. (Notice whether everything is being underlined on your monitor as you type.)

This text was typed with AUTO UNDERLINE-TEXT MODE.

Exit the Auto Underline-Text mode now by holding Alt and pressing the hyphen/underline key once. Notice the S↓N↓ is returned to its normal state. Press return twice.

When you tap the space bar while in Auto Underline-Text mode, a line with no characters above it will be created. This would be useful for typing ruled tables or for typing forms or questionnaires in which you need long lines with no words above them.

Press Alt and the hyphen/underline key now to get into Auto Underline-Text mode. Then tap the space bar to create a line. Toggle out of Auto-Underline Text mode the same way you got into it, by pressing Alt and hyphen/underline.

To deunderline or erase the underline in screen text, place your cursor on any text that has been underlined. Then hold down the shift key while you tap the hyphen/underline key. This deunderlines or deletes the underline but not the text above it. To try this, place your cursor on the word *This* and deunderline the text through space after the word *with*. Press End and two returns.

AUTO UNDERLINE-ALPHANUMERIC

In addition to the Auto Underline-Text function, there is the Auto Underline-Alphanumeric function. The only two differences are in what they do and how they are activated. Auto Underline-Alphanumeric underlines only letters and numbers, it does not underline punctuation and spaces. To access Auto Underline-Alphanumeric, use Alt and the equals/plus key.

Press Alt and the equals/plus key to try the function now. Type the following sentence:

This sentence was typed in Auto Underline-Alphanumeric mode.

Exit the Auto Underline-Alphanumeric mode by pressing Alt and the equals/plus key. Note: spaces and punctuation were not underlined. Press return twice.

SUPERSCRIPT AND SUBSCRIPT

Superscript makes alphanumeric characters print one-half line higher than the rest of the line such as for footnote reference numbers. Subscript makes characters print one-half line lower, as in H_2O. Some printers may not be able to accommodate these functions, so check your printer manual if they don't work.

Superscript characters are created by activating the Superscript function key, Alt-Q, in the space before the character to be raised. ↑ should appear on the screen. Subscript characters are created with the Subscript function key, Alt-W, which places ↓ on the screen. *Note:* These arrows do not show up on the printed copy.

When you type a superscript character, you must follow it with a subscript character to bring the rest of the line back to the level of the regular writing line. Conversely, you must follow a subscript with a superscript. Here is an example. To type H_2O, first type *H*, then Alt-W (for subscript). Now type *2*, because you wish to have it as a subscript character. To raise the line back to the regular level, type Alt-Q (for superscript), and then type *O*. On the screen you will see *H↓2↑O*.

Try typing the following superscripts and subscripts on your screen now. (Space five times between items.)

$H_2O \quad 10b^2 + 4a^2 \quad 40°F. \quad footnote^5$

Be sure every up arrow has a corresponding down arrow and vice versa.

ENDING THIS SESSION

If you want to stop your work on the computer for now, press F10 to save the document and exit to the Main Menu. If you want to continue this session, leave your document on the screen and turn to Chapter 8 where you will learn how to print it.

SUMMARY OF OPERATIONS COVERED IN THIS CHAPTER

Center

1. Place the cursor at the beginning of the writing line.
2. Press F3 and type the line to be centered.
3. End the Center function by pressing return.

Indent

1. Set a tab in the format line at the column to which you want lines indented.
2. Put the cursor at beginning of the writing line.
3. Press F4 and type the line using wraparound.
4. End the Indent function by pressing return.

Decimal Tabs

1. Set tabs in the format line at columns in which you want the decimals to appear.

2. Put the cursor at left edge of the writing line.
3. Press shift-F4 to activate the Decimal Tab function.
4. Type the items to be aligned.
5. Dec Tab to a new column or press return to end the line.

Hardspaces (Required Spaces)

1. Place the cursor where you want the hardspace.
2. Use Alt-S instead of the space bar.

Auto Underline-Text and Auto Underline-Alphanumeric

1. Place the cursor where the underlined text is to begin.
2. Press Alt and the hyphen/underline key to get into Auto Underline-Text mode or press Alt and the equals/plus key to get into Auto Underline Alphanumeric mode.
3. Type the text you want underlined.
4. Press the space bar while in Auto Underline-Text mode for a line with no text above it.
5. Toggle out of either Auto Underline-mode by simultaneously pressing Alt and the hyphen/underline key or Alt and the equals/plus key.

Deunderline

1. Put the cursor on the underline you want removed. (You may or may not be in Auto Underline mode.)
2. Hold down the shift key and press the hyphen/underline key to the remove the line. Text above the line will not be affected.

Superscript

1. Put the cursor on the space before the one where the superscript character will appear.
2. Press Alt-Q.
3. Type the character to be raised.
4. Press Alt-W to bring the line back down.

Subscript

1. Put the cursor on the space before the one where the subscript character is to appear.
2. Tap Alt-W.
3. Type the character to be lowered.
4. Tap Alt-Q to bring the line back up to the regular writing line.

8

PRINTING A DOCUMENT

One of the most important activities you will perform with MultiMate is printing. After all, your primary task in word processing is producing a printed document; or, in word processing jargon, a *hard copy.*

For several reasons printing can sometimes be troublesome. First, *interfacing,* or coordinating, your computer with a printer is often complicated because usually the printer is made by a different manufacturer. At last count, over 100 models of printers have been used with MultiMate. Second, a printer is composed of many moving parts that can break down. Finally, your printer might not be as sophisticated as the MultiMate program. For example, it may not be capable of printing superscript, subscript, boldface print, etc.

Since this book can't possibly give instructions for all of the printers with which MultiMate can be used, you will need to rely on the instruction manual that came with your printer. If you have difficulty, consult the vendor who sold you the printer, and finally, the MultiMate support service whose toll free number is in your MultiMate user manual.

A WORD ABOUT TERMINOLOGY

In this chapter you will see the terms *spool, spooling statistics,* and *spool queue.* Spooling allows MultiMate to complete operations more efficiently by allowing it to place documents to be printed in a *queue* (lineup). The documents in a spool queue are printed in the order in which they were submitted.

MultiMate allows you to line up as many as 30 documents to be printed. You can then use the screen for other operations (such as editing) while the documents in the spool queue continue printing. Although you can remove them from the spool queue, documents will typically remain there until the system prints them, until you turn the system off, or until you press Ctrl, Alt, and Del to restart the system.

READYING THE PRINTER

From your printer manual, obtain specific instructions on how to load the paper and turn on the printer. Be sure it is ready for the print command you will soon be sending.

ACCESSING THE PRINTING PROCESS

There are two ways to access the printing process. Follow the procedure that fits your current situation: if the Main Menu is on your screen, use procedure a. and if the document FEATURES is on your screen, use procedure b.

> a. With the Main Menu on your screen, type 3 for *Print Document Utility,* and press return. This gives you the PRINT A DOCUMENT screen on which you are asked to name the document you want to print. The default document drive appears automatically, but you could change it if you want to print a document stored on a drive other than the default document drive.
>
> You will now print the document you created in Chapter 7. Type the name, *FEATURES,* after *Document:*. (You may use either upper- or lowercase; the system will automatically convert lowercase to uppercase for you.) Follow the screen prompts until the Submit a Document for Printing screen appears.
>
> b. To print a document currently on your screen, press Alt-3. You will skip over the Print a Document screen directly to the Submit a Document for Printing screen. This saves time because you don't have to save the document and exit to the Main Menu. You don't even have to type the name of the document. When you press Alt-3, the document is automatically saved to the disk.

Note: You can access *any* Main Menu function from within a document by pressing Alt and the correct number of the Main Menu function. For example, pressing Alt-1 will start the Edit an Old Document process so you can edit another document. The document that was on the screen is automatically saved to disk.
No matter which process you used, the Submit a Document for Printing screen should now be displayed.

THE SUBMIT A DOCUMENT FOR PRINTING SCREEN

The Submit a Document for Printing screen is shown in Figure 8.1, and each field of this screen is explained below. Notice that each has a *default,* or preset value. You can change these if they don't match your specifications. The values in effect when you finally print will be stored with the document. They will appear instead of the system default values the next time you print the document. Type *Y* if you want to answer *yes* to a default question; type *N* if you want to answer *no.*

Now tab to move the cursor to each field and read the explanations about each as you go. (If you wanted to advance the cursor more rapidly, you could use the cursor-moving keys rather than tab.)

At the top of the screen you will see the drive on which the document is stored: Drive: B. The name *FEATURES* appears after the word *Document:.*

Note: Follow the pattern of the defaults when you change them. For example, if a default is 001, use a three digit number when you change it. If the default is a date shown as 01:06:85, use the same pattern and number of digits.

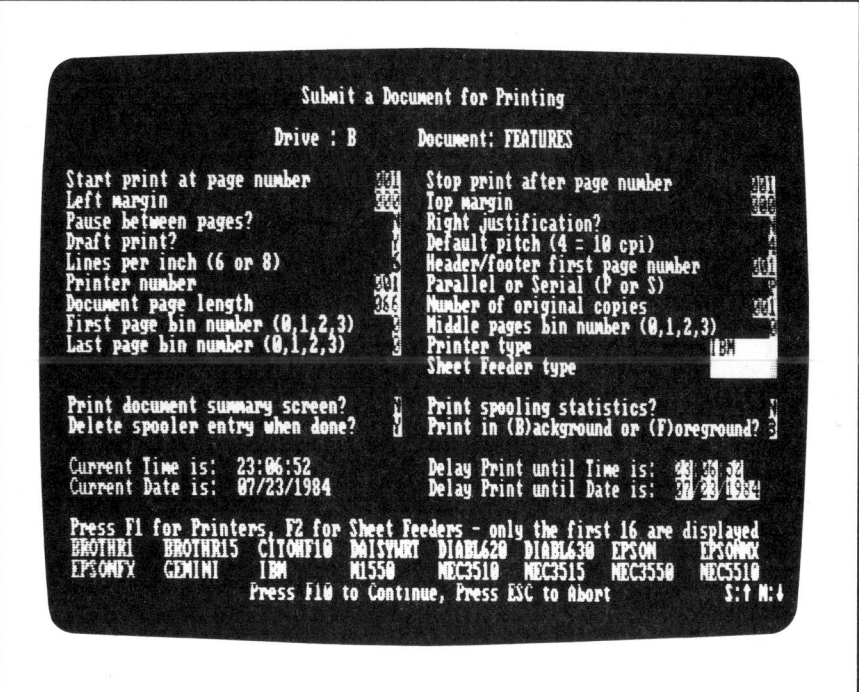

Figure 8.1 – *Submit a Document for Printing screen.*

At the top of the left column the screen says *Start print at page number,* with a default of 001. The top of the right hand column says *Stop print at page number* with a default equal to the number of pages in your document. These numbers indicate the first and last pages to be printed. If you want all of the pages printed, leave the defaults. In this case, FEATURES has only one page, so leave these settings as they are.

Here is the big advantage of this feature. If you notice you made an error on page six of a ten-page document, you can use *Edit an Old Document* to correct it, and then print only page six again. All you have to do is change the values: *Start print at page number* to *006,* and *Stop print at page number* to *006.*

The next line says *Left margin;* its default is 000. You must enter a three digit number to indicate how many spaces in from the left edge of the paper your writing line should begin printing.

Here's how to figure out where to set your left margin. The pitch size will determine how many columns or characters wide the paper is. For example, pitch size 5 is 12 characters per inch (*cpi*). (See Figure 8.3 for other possibilites.) If your paper is 8½ inches wide (standard size), multiply 8½ × 12 cpi to get 102 columns.

Assume your writing line in FEATURES was the preset 75 spaces wide. So, there will be 27 total spaces in margins (102 − 75 = 27). Half of these margin spaces belong on each side (27 ÷ 2 = 13½). Round this to 14 spaces for a left margin.

For pica type (10 cpi or pitch = 4), a sheet of standard 8½-inch wide paper is only 85 spaces wide because the letters are larger. For a 75-space pica writing line, there will be ten total spaces in margins (85 − 75 = 10). Since you want half the margin spaces on each side, use half of 10 or 5 spaces for a left margin. When you use a 75-space writing line with pica type size, set 005 for a left margin.

You never *set* a right margin. The right margin will always equal the left margin plus the number of spaces in the writing line. *Note:* Be careful not to exceed the column width capacity of your printer, or else the lines will wrap around and print the excess characters to the left of your left margin. Figure 8.2 shows you what this would look like.

Now set a left margin of 014 or 005, depending upon which pitch size you will use (some printers have only one).

```
         lect a left         If you use a writing line that is 75 spaces wide and then se
         ch) on the          margin of 020 and a default pitch of 4 (10 characters per in
                             Submit a Document For Printing Menu, this will be the result
```

Figure 8.2 – Exceeding the width capability of the printer

Top margin is the next field; it also has a default of 000. Enter a three-digit number to indicate the number of lines you want left blank at the top of every page.

For example, a standard 8½ × 11-inch piece of paper has 66 lines. If your page is a full 54 lines, you specify 006 for the top margin. Thus, printing will end on line 60 of 66 possible lines. This would leave a bottom margin of six lines or one inch.

In this case, type *006* so that FEATURES will begin printing one inch down. Next, *Pause between pages?* asks if you want the printer to stop so you can insert a new sheet of paper or adjust the top margin on continuous form paper. Type *Y* if you wish the printer to stop after each page. A screen prompt will instruct you to press Esc to continue. (Check your printer manual to see if you must do anything special to the printer before making adjustments to the paper.) When you leave the default at *N,* the printer will continue after each page. The *Pause between pages?* function works in both foreground and background printing modes, which are explained later in this chapter. Leave the default, *N,* since FEATURES is only one page long.

Right justification? If you leave the default *N,* an uneven right margin will be printed. If you change the default to *Y,* the system will insert extra spaces between words so that the right edges of lines not ending in returns will be aligned. Don't change the default this time.

Draft print? Y causes the printer to print single strike characters; *N* instructs the printer to print double strike. Double strike means that characters are printed twice to make them darker. You can have a document printed with single strike characters, then have additional commands before and after those words you want printed with double strike. These commands are explained in Chapter 9. Leave the setting on *N* for FEATURES.

Default pitch (4 = 10 cpi): Pitch refers to the number of characters printed per horizontal inch or *cpi*. The default is *4* which indicates you want 10 characters per inch. Refer to the chart below for typical examples of cpi which will result from various pitch settings. Exact results depend on which printer you are using. Some printers may be capable of only one pitch size.

Your printer instruction manual will also provide information about which pitch sizes are possible; usually if you use one that isn't available, the closest available one will be substituted. Choose a pitch appropriate for your printer at this time.

Lines per inch (6 or 8): You can choose to have 6 or 8 lines printed in a vertical inch. The default value is *6,* which is standard vertical spacing on most typewriters. Your other choice, 8 lines per inch, would make the vertical lines closer together. Leave the default for now.

Header/footer first page number: The Header/Footer function (covered in Chapter 14) automatically numbers pages. If you want the first page number to be 1, use the default, *001*. But, you can

```
Pitch Setting        Resulting Characters Per Inch
     1                         5      (the largest characters
                                       or fewest cpi of which
                                       the printer is capable)
     2                         6
     3                         8.5
     4                        10      (comparable to pica type)
     5                        12      (comparable to elite type)
     6                        13.2
     7                        15
     8                        16.5
     9                        17.6    (the smallest characters
                                       or most cpi of which the
                                       printer is capable)
```

Figure 8.3 – Pitch sizes

begin numbering with any page number; just type in the three digit number to indicate your choice. You did not set up headers or footers in FEATURES so don't worry about this field now.

Printer number: The default is *001*. If you have more than one printer attached to your system, you can send the print command to the one you want. For example, you might have a dot matrix printer (for speedy rough drafts) and a daisy wheel printer (for letter quality documents). Your computer manual and your printer manual will have details about how to set this up. If you have only one printer, leave the default, *001*.

Parallel or serial (P or S): The default P stands for *parallel port,* and it indicates the method used to transfer data to the printer. The method is determined by the printer you are using, so refer to your printer manual before choosing.

Document page length: This indicates the number of lines (at the rate of six per inch) on the paper you are using. The default is *066*, which is the number of vertical lines on standard paper, ll inches long. The printer uses this number to determine how far to roll down when rolling out a single sheet or when feeding continuous form paper. Leave the default set on *066*.

Number of original copies: The default is *001*. If you wanted more than one copy of the document printed, you would change the default value to the number of copies you need. Just print one copy of FEATURES.

The *First page bin number (0,1,2,3),* the *Middle pages bin number (0,1,2,3),* and the *Last page bin number (0,1,2,3)* defaults at *0* must be changed if you are using a *sheet feeder.* It is a device that automatically feeds paper to your printer. The default of *0* tells the system that you are not using a sheet feeder.

If you are using a sheet feeder, indicate with a *1, 2,* or *3* the bin number which contains the type of paper you want used for the first page of your document (e.g. letterhead), the middle, and all but first and last pages (e.g. plain bond), and the last page. Make a correct selection for this field now.

Printer type: Here you indicate the printer you will be using. When you press F1, you will see at the bottom of the screen a list of *printer action tables* (PATs) available on your system disk. PATs are files that contain the codes that make the printer operate properly.

The default, TTYCRLF, is a generic printer action table. You can use this default when your specific printer is not named in the list of PATs. It may not enable your printer to do all of the fancy printing functions such as superscript and subscript, variable pitches, enhanced and draft print, etc., but it will allow it to do the basics.

To see the PATs available on this disk, tap F1. If you want to name a table other than the default, TTYCRLF, use strikeover to type the name of the PAT that works with your printer. If the new name is shorter than the default name, delete the extra characters with Del. Leave TTYCRLF or type in the name of your PAT now.

Sheet Feeder type: There is no default here. If you are using a sheet feeder, type the name of it here now. Press F2 to see a list of sheet feeder action tables (like PATs) on your disk.

Print document summary screen? The default is *N*. If you type *Y* here, the *Document Summary Screen* will be printed before the document. It shows the document name, author, addressee, operator, identification key words, comments, creation date, and modification date. If you keep a hard copy of your documents, you might also want to keep a copy of their Document Summary screens. Leave the default *N* for now.

Print spooling statistics? Spooling statistics are the items on this Submit a Document for Printing screen showing the choices you made to print the document. If you type *Y* this screen will be printed. The default is *N*, since you usually don't need to have this screen printed. Leave the default *N* for now.

Delete spooler entry when done? The default is *Y*. If you type *N*, the document will be left on the spool queue after it is printed. This means it will be left lined up at the printer but on hold. It can be printed again by releasing it from hold, a process described in Chapter 9. Leave the default *Y* in the blank so FEATURES will be automatically removed from the spool queue and saved to the disk after it is printed.

Print in (B)ackground or (F)oreground? If you press *B*, you can edit one document while printing another. This is called printing in the *background*. It is especially efficient when you use continuous form paper fed on a tractor feed, because while the document prints unattended, you can use the screen.

If you press *F*, you will have more control for printing but will not be able to do anything else on the screen. In *foreground* printing, the system stops printing after each page so you can insert another single sheet. Printing resumes when you press the Esc key as instructed by the screen prompt. Type *F* for print in foreground this time.

Current Time is: and *Current Date is:* If you entered the correct date and time when you loaded MultiMate, these two lines will automatically reflect the current date and time. If you tapped return instead of entering the values when loading, a preprogrammed (but possibly incorrect) date and time appear as default values. You cannot enter a new date and time here.

Delay Print until Time is: and *Delay Print until Date is:* These default to the same numbers which appear in the lines discussed above. If you want to delay printing for some reason, enter the date and time at which you want printing to begin. If you share a printer, you could specify a time for the printer to begin.

If you press F10 and printing doesn't start immediately, check this field to be sure printing hasn't been delayed. Now press F10 to send the command to the printer, and go to the printer to retrieve your first hard copy!

Note: Since there were a variety of writing line widths in the document FEATURES, lines which you centered may not appear centered in this printed copy.

SUMMARY OF OPERATIONS COVERED IN THIS CHAPTER

Printing a Document

1. Access the Submit a Document for Printing screen:
   a. From the Main Menu, press 3, return, and type the name of the document to be printed.
   b. From within the document you want to print, tap Alt-3.

2. When on the Submit a Document for Printing screen, be sure each of the fields is filled in properly.

3. Be sure the printer is ready.

4. Press F10.

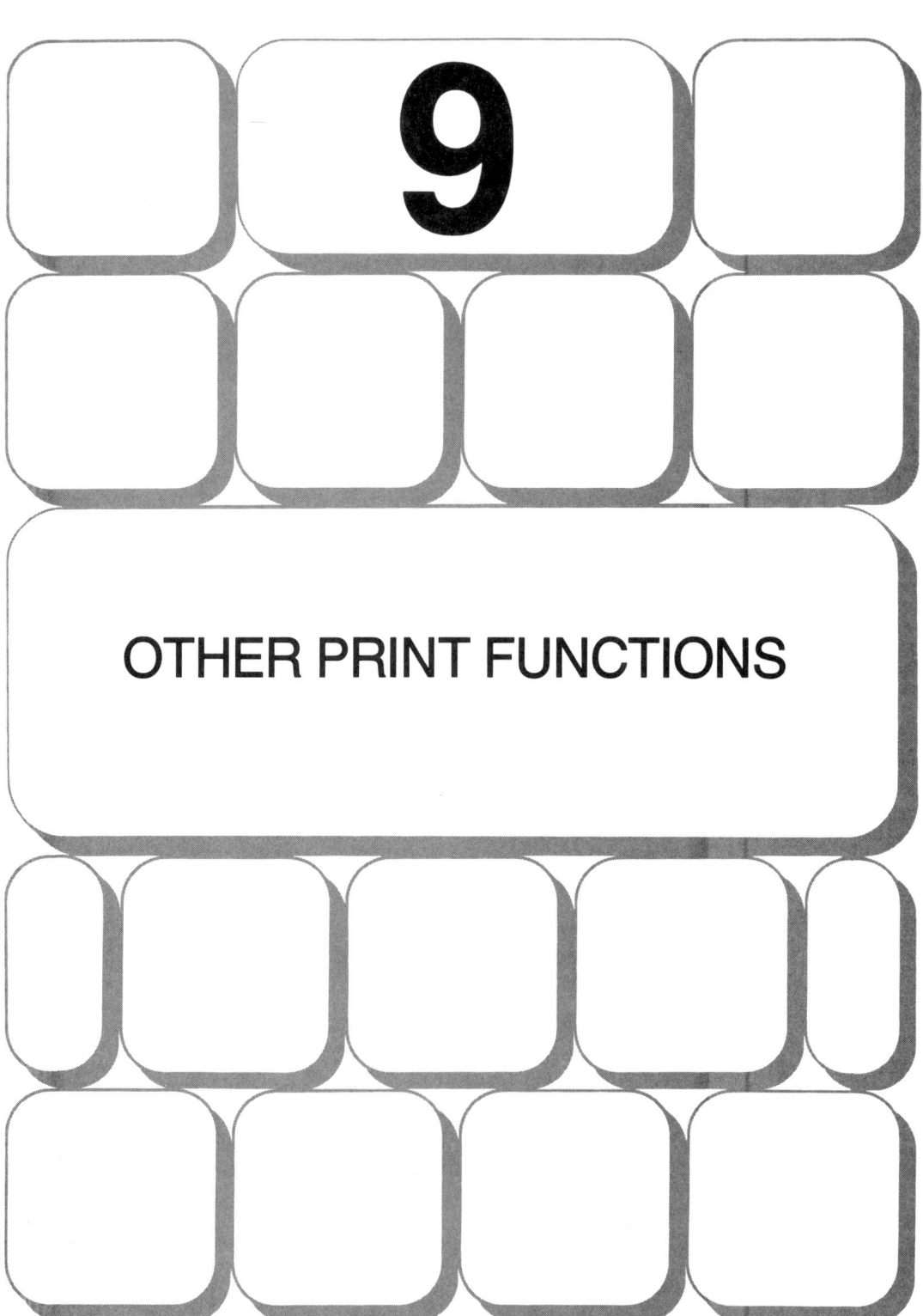

9

OTHER PRINT FUNCTIONS

Other Print Functions 93

This chapter covers additional printer-related functions such as printing from the screen, stopping printing, and using special print modes and printer utilities.

Get ready to try the operations in this chapter by making sure the Main Menu is on your screen now.

THE PRINT SCREEN KEY

The Print Screen key provides another way to print. It prints line by line exactly what is on the screen. Every character which your printer is capable of printing, including the format line, screen symbols such as tabs and returns, etc., will be printed.

You wouldn't use Print Screen for printing final copies of business letters, but you could use it as a quick alternative for short rough drafts, notes to yourself, or copies of menus you want to study at home when you are first learning the system.

Before you use the Print Screen function, be sure the printer is on and ready to print. The Print Screen key is labelled PrtSc and is located to the right of the right shift key. Press shift-PrtSc now. The printer should immediately begin printing the Main Menu screen line by line. When it has finished printing, advance and remove the paper with the method described in your manual.

STOPPING PRINTING TEMPORARILY

There are three ways to stop and restart printing.

The first way is to include a Pause Printer instruction in text as you type it. You might need to change a daisy wheel to a different type style, or you might want to stop the printer after each zip code in a list of names and addresses to insert a new envelope.

Try Pause Printer now. From the Main Menu, use Edit an Old Document procedures to get the document FEATURES on the screen once more. Pick a point about halfway through the page at which you will make the printer pause. Place the cursor at this point and press Alt-P. The Pause Printer symbol (⌂) will display on the screen. This symbol doesn't show up or take up space on the printed page, so when you place it between two words, you will also need a space between them. Insert a space with the + key, if needed.

Now use the Alt-3 procedure you learned in Chapter 8 to print the document currently on the screen. Be sure the printer and the paper are ready before pressing the final F10.

Printing will stop at the Pause Printer symbol. When you are ready to resume printing, follow the screen prompt which instructs you to: *Press Esc to Continue*. Print the rest of the page; the Main Menu should then be on the screen.

You can use a Pause Printer symbol in either background or foreground print modes. (Unfortunately, with some dot matrix printers, printing pauses at the beginning of the line rather than at the exact point of the Pause Print symbol.)

The second method of stopping a printer after it has already started printing is to tap the printer's ON LINE button. Printing will stop and after a short time, the following prompt will appear on the screen: *Printer Needs Attention. Press <ESC> to Continue*. When you are ready to proceed, tap Esc. To resume printing, tap the ON LINE button again.

Note: Although this method is typical for most printers, check your printer manual to be sure it will work properly on your printer.

A third way to temporarily stop printing (by placing the document on hold) will be covered later in this chapter in a discussion of the Printer Queue Control.

STOPPING PRINTING PERMANENTLY

When you want to stop a document from printing permanently, use one of these two methods.

If a document is printing in *foreground* mode, stop printing by tapping the Esc key. Printing will immediately stop, the paper will advance automatically, and the Main Menu will be displayed.

Since that is a fairly straightforward procedure, let's practice instead on the procedure used for stopping a document that is printing in the background. First, from the Main Menu, use choice 3 to send the document named FEATURES to the printer. (Be sure you tell the printer to print in the background mode.)

You stop printing by pressing Ctrl and tapping the Break key which is located in the upper right hand corner of the keyboard. The screen then displays the Printer Queue Control menu as shown in Figure 9.3. Check the lower right corner of the screen. If *CTRL* is displayed there, press Ctrl again. If *S↓ N↓* is displayed, continue. Place the cursor by the name of the document (if it isn't already there) and press 1 and then F10 to remove the document from the spool queue. This permanently cancels your request to print the document. More information is given on this method later in this chapter under Printer Queue Control. Follow screen prompts to return to the Main Menu.

If your printer has a *buffer,* a device in which some or all of a document is held until it is printed, printing may not stop immediately. Once text is in this buffer, it will be printed regardless of your request because it is no longer under the control of the computer. Your printer manual should explain the buffer and how to clear it.

SPECIAL PRINT MODES

If your printer will support them, there are three degrees of darkness available in printed characters. If your printer is capable of only one, *single strike* (also called *draft* mode), is automatically selected. There is a second level of printing, *double strike* or *enhanced* mode, and a third level, *bold* print, which doubles the effect of single and double strike. You can also create *shadow print,* which creates the look of a shadow under each character. Figure 9.1 explains all of the special printing modes.

Your document is printed with either single (draft) or double strike (enhanced) mode as you specify in the *Draft Print: Y or N* field on the Submit a Document for Printing screen. If you want to have some characters printed darker, you must insert commands to override the mode specified for the rest of the document.

Let's now create a document that will show samples of the special print modes available on your own printer.

With the Main Menu on your screen, press 2 and return to create a new document called SAMPLES. Follow the screen prompts to get

PRINT MODE	KEYS TO START	SCREEN SYMBOL	KEYS TO STOP	SCREEN SYMBOL	EFFECT
Draft (single strike)	Alt-D		Alt-N		regular, single struck text (overrides enhanced print setting)
Enhanced (double strike)	Alt-N		Alt-D		double struck text (overrides draft print setting)
Bold	Alt-Z		Alt-Z		any print mode currently in effect will be double struck
Shadow Print	Alt-X		Alt-X		characters are printed once, then again, slightly off-set from the first printing (creates a shadow effect)

Figure 9.1 – Special printing modes

to the first page. Then type sentences that name the printing modes and set each up so the name will be printed in the specified mode. For example, in the sentence *Here is an example of enhanced print,* set up the last two words of that sentence to be printed in enhanced print mode. Repeat the procedure for each type of print and print out this document for later reference. You should print the reference sheet twice. On one page, type *This page was printed with draft print :y,* and on the other type *This page was printed with draft print :N* (or enhanced print).

For your first example, enhanced print, follow the steps in the next paragraph. *Note:* in this section (sp) means press the space bar.

Type *Here is an example of*(sp). The cursor is now at the location where enhanced printing is to begin. Press Alt-N to start the enhanced print mode. You will see the screen symbol (∩). Now type *Enhanced print*(sp). Next, stop the enhanced print. Your cursor is where you want draft print to begin again, so press Alt-D. You will see the draft print symbol (δ). Finish the sentence by typing the word *mode.*

Remember, the screen symbols indicating the starting or stopping of any of the special print modes don't print out or take up printed spaces. When you insert them, you must type spaces before and after the words, or they will be run together on the printed sheet.

The chart in Figure 9.1 shows the key combinations, symbols, and effect of each of the special print modes. Now type an example of each in your document.

Note: These special print modes are possible only if your printer is capable of doing them. Read your printer manual before attempting to use them.

Bold print doubles whatever mode is in effect. So, a bold print command inserted into a document in which you selected *Draft Print? N* on the Submit a Document for Printing screen (thus making it print in double strike or enhanced print) is going to create quad struck characters.

Bold print is a special mode. It will not work with your system's extended character set (e.g. special graphics characters). Also, bold printing should not be followed with shadow print, tab, indent, etc., because this juxtaposition causes problems for the printer.

After typing a sentence for each printing mode, return a couple of times, and leave the document on the screen for the next section.

CHANGING PITCH WITHIN A DOCUMENT

On the Submit a Document for Printing screen (see Figure 8.1, Chapter 8) you specified a default pitch from 1 to 9 for your document. In much the same way and for the same reasons as special print modes were inserted into the text, *pitch* can be changed. You usually do this for emphasis.

To instruct the printer to change pitch, place the cursor before the characters to be changed and press Alt-C (the Print Pitch function key combination) and the number corresponding to the desired pitch. (In Figure 8.3, you see a chart of pitch settings and the number of characters per inch that will result if your printer is capable of them.)

To change the pitch back to its original size or to a different one, again press Alt-C and type the setting that will give you the number of characters per inch you want.

Accessing Printer Control Utilities

A *utility* is any special function performed by a computer. There are two utilities associated with printing that you access from the Main Menu. Press 4 and return from the Main Menu, to see the screen shown in Figure 9.2.

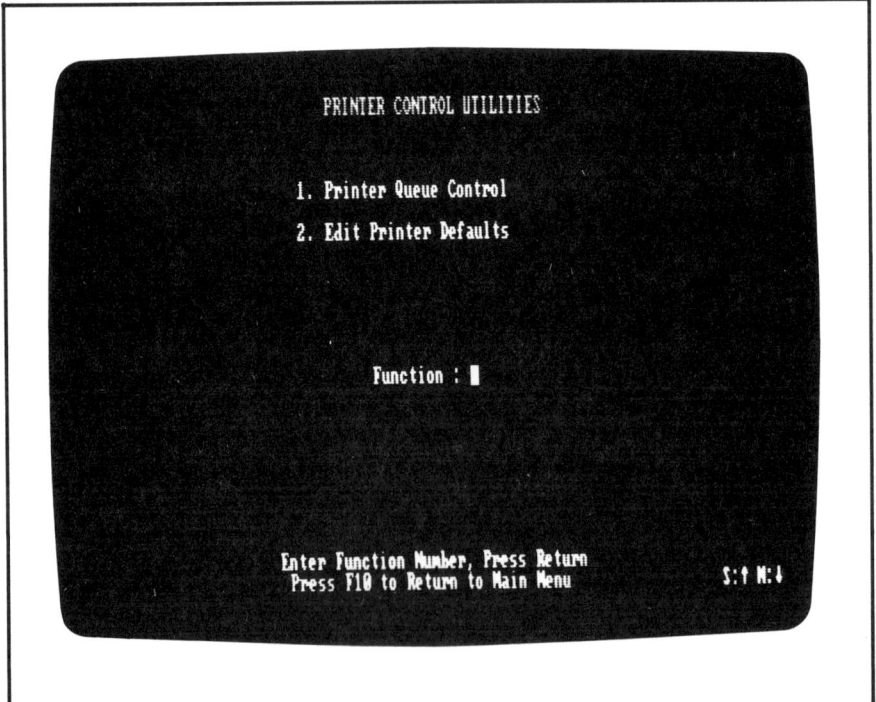

Figure 9.2 – *Printer control utilities*

1. Printer Queue Control

Now press 1 and return. You will arrive at the Print Queue Control screen shown in Figure 9.3. From here, you can manipulate the documents that are queued (lined up) at the printer.

Names of documents queued to the printer will be displayed at mid screen. The display method used shows whether your document is printing, on hold, or in error status. If the name of your document is shown in the same display method as the word *hold,* then your document is on *hold,* i.e. not being printed. If the name of your document is blinking, it is in *error status.* This usually occurs if you send a command to print before the printer has been turned on.

Here is description of each of the five options available on the Printer Queue Control menu.

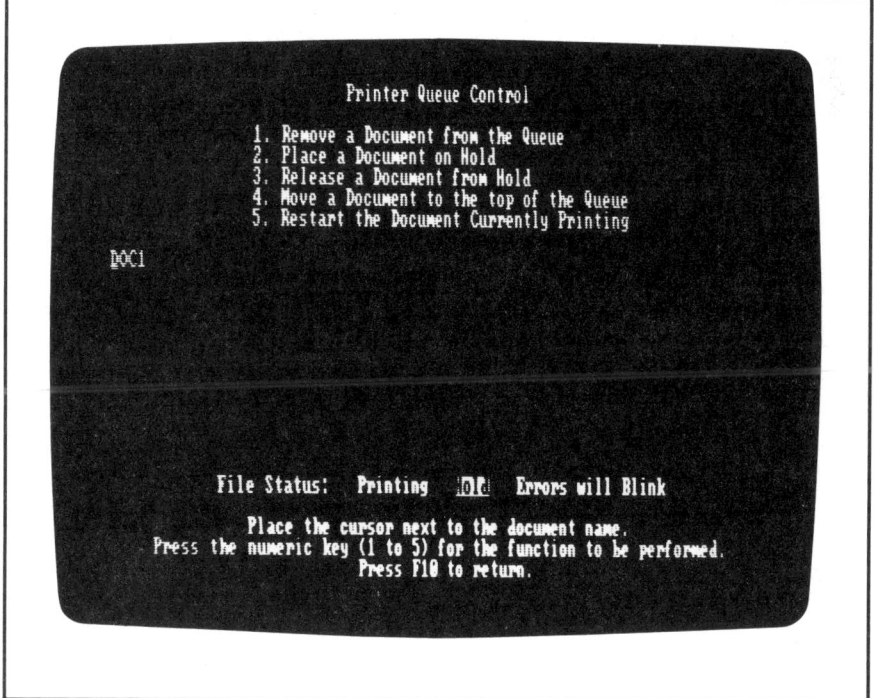

Figure 9.3 – Printer queue control

1. *Remove a Document from the Queue* If you press 1, you cancel a previous request to print. The document will not be printed until you send another request.

2. *Place a Document on Hold* Press 2 to take a document out of the printer lineup temporarily. You can reinstate it by using the next option. Although it is not in line to be printed, a document on hold could not be edited before you removed it from the queue completely with option 1.

3. *Release a Document from Hold* This puts the document back in the line to be printed in its turn.

4. *Move a Document to the top of the Queue* Press 4 to change the order of the lineup so that the document on which the cursor was placed will be printed next.

5. *Restart the Document Currently Printing* If the printer stops because it runs out of paper, for example, you can press 5 to restart it.

To request any of these changes, select the document to be affected by placing the cursor beside its name. All documents in the print queue are listed mid screen. Then tap the number of the option you want and press F10. Follow the screen prompts to return to the Main Menu.

2. Edit Printer Defaults

Your second choice on the Printer Control Utilities menu is *Edit Printer Defaults.* If you press 2 and return, you will see the Modify Printer Defaults menu. Figure 9.4 shows this menu.

Most of the same fields from the Submit a Document for Printing screen appear here. You will see the default (preset) values and have the option of changing them permanently. This allows you to customize the system to the settings you use most often.

For example, you can change the *Printer Type* to the name of your printer so that you won't have to type it in each time you submit a document for printing. Or, you may prefer to have all or most of your documents printed with a justified right margin. In this case, change the default for *Right justification?* to *Y.*

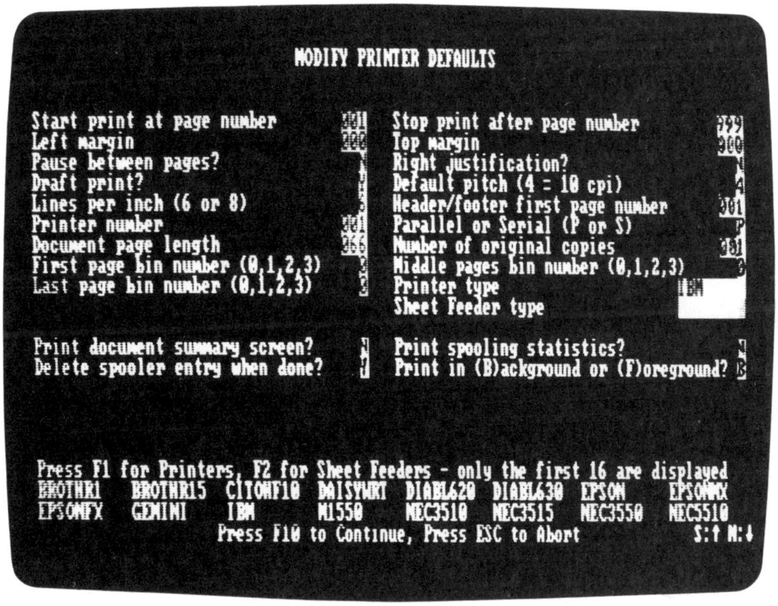

Figure 9.4 – Modify Printer Defaults screen

SUMMARY OF OPERATIONS COVERED IN THIS CHAPTER

Stopping Printing Temporarily—Pause Print

1. Place the cursor under the character after which you want the printer to pause.
2. Press Alt-P. (Insert space if necessary.)
3. After printing stops, Esc will start the printer again as a screen prompt will remind you.

Stopping Printing Temporarily—The ON LINE Button

1. Press the printer ON LINE button once to stop printing.
2. Press the ON LINE button again to resume printing.

Stopping Printing Permanently (Background Print Mode)

1. Press Ctrl-Break.
2. The Printer Queue Control menu displays.
3. Place your cursor by the name of the document you want to stop (if it isn't already there).
4. Press 1 and then F10 to cancel the print order.

Stopping Printing Permanently (Foreground Print Mode)

1. Press Esc. Then wait for the buffer to empty.

Setting up Special Print Modes

1. Press the key combination for the type of print mode you want to start.
2. Type the words to be affected.
3. Press the key combination which stops the special print mode by starting another mode.

Changing Pitch within a Document

1. Place the cursor on the character before the pitch change.
2. Press Alt-C and type the number of the new pitch.
3. Keyboard the characters you want to be printed in the different pitch.
4. To end the new pitch mode, repeat steps 1–3.

Accessing the Printer Queue Control

1. From the Main Menu, press 4 and return.
2. From the Printer Control Utilities screen, press 1 and return.

3. Choose one of the five options by placing the cursor on the name of the document you want affected. Press a number from 1–5 to indicate the option you choose, and press F10.
4. Follow screen prompts to the Main Menu.

Accessing the Editing Printer Defaults

1. From the Main Menu, press 4 and return.
2. From the Printer Control Utilities screen, press 2 and return.
3. Use strikeover to change the defaults.
4. Follow screen prompts to the Main Menu.

10

ADVANCED EDITING FUNCTIONS THAT RELOCATE TEXT: MOVE, COPY, AND EXTERNAL COPY

The Move, Copy, and External Copy functions covered in this chapter are advanced editing functions. They involve manipulation of larger amounts of text, require greater thought and planning, and contain more steps than the previous functions. Move, Copy, and External Copy all require highlighting (covered in Chapter 4).

For any function, whether it is simple or complex, remember:

- what the function is designed to do;
- where to place the cursor before beginning the function;
- how to initiate the function (access the Help facility with shift-F1 if you forget).

It is unnecessary to memorize each step of these more complicated functions. The same key you used to initiate the function is generally used to make the function continue. You can follow the screen prompts for additional help.

Note: To stop any of these functions before they are completed, press Esc. When the operation is stopped, the cursor will return to its original location.

Let's now take a look at these functions one by one.

THE MOVE FUNCTION

The Move function takes text from one location in a document and puts it in another location in the same document. Material will be erased from its original position. Compare Figure 10.1 (before moving text) and Figure 10.2 (after moving text). The Move function exchanged the order of the paragraphs. To see how this works, type the material in Figure 10.1 in a new document named MOVE.

The symbols in this sample are ≪ for return, ≫ for tabs, for the Center instruction, and ϕ for hard spaces.

To accomplish the move (switch the order of the paragraphs), put the cursor on the first character or symbol to be moved, ≪ after the title. Press F7, the Move function key, and *Move What?* appears on screen.

<->PLAN FOR HIRING NEW EMPLOYEES FOR THE SAN FRANCISCO DIVISION

<<

>>Our goal is to have completed the hiring process for the following openings in our new SF@facility no later than November@30. We will need a WP@Supervisor, two WP@Operators, a DP@Manager, and a computer operator. All other new employees will be transferred to the SF@Division from either Plant@2 or Plant@3 in Seattle. <<

<<

>>To have the new people interviewed, hired, and on board by November@30, the preliminary hiring process must be begun no later than August@30. For help in scheduling the process, please contact Ann Werckman in Seattle; she is our personnel consultant. <<

<<

Figure 10.1 – Before moving text

<<

<<

       <->PLAN FOR HIRING NEW EMPLOYEES FOR THE SAN FRANCISCO DIVISION<<

<<

>>To have the new people interviewed, hired, and on board by November@30, the preliminary hiring process must be begun no later than August@30. For help in scheduling the process, please contact Ann Werckman in Seattle; she is our personnel consultant. <<

<<

>>Our goal is to have completed the hiring process for the following openings in our new SF@facility no later than November@30. We will need a WP@Supervisor, two WP@Operators, a DP@Manager, and a computer operator.

All other new employees will be transferred to the SF@Division from either Plant@2 or Plant@3 in Seattle. <<

<<

Figure 10.2 – *After moving text*

Next, highlight all of the characters you want to move. Determine if you need to move the returns, tabs, etc. as well as the text; in most cases, you will move these along with the text. Tap return here to move this entire paragraph.

If you want to move the format line with the text, press the Format key (F9). If you don't move the format line, the text will conform to the format line in existence at the new location. In this case, we don't need to change the format line, so don't press F9.

Press the Move key (F7) again to indicate that everything has been highlighted. Notice that the screen prompt *To Where?* appears in the upper right hand corner.

Now indicate where you want the material to be moved. To do this, put the cursor on the first character that will *follow* the material after it is moved. In this example, place the cursor under the return graphic below the last line in the second paragraph. Finally, press the Move key (F7) one last time to complete the move.

Note: Some planning may be required to avoid having to edit after a move is completed. The paragraph you just moved began with a return on a line by itself, which created a blank line between the paragraphs. This return will now provide a blank line after the title.

Save and exit the document by pressing F10.

USES OF THE MOVE FUNCTION

Move is very handy when you want to reorganize your text. Before word processing, writers had to "cut and paste" with scissors and tape.

Move is useful if you like to compose at the keyboard or think out loud with a dictation unit microphone in your hand. You can be initially concerned only with getting those thoughts down; it's simple to put them in a better arrangement later without retyping.

THE COPY FUNCTION

The Copy function is very similar to the Move function. The difference is that after a Copy, the material both moves to the new location *and* stays in the same place.

The text in Figure 10.3 shows the material *before* it is copied in Figure 10.4.

To see how Copy works, create a new document called COPY and type the material in Figure 10.3. Before beginning, set tabs at spaces 12, 27, and 53. Do not type the *A* or *B* at the edge of the blank lines; they are for reference only.

Now copy the lines in the example in Figure 10.3. First, put the cursor on the first character of the material you want copied: the first character of the blank lines marked with the A. Tap the Copy key (F8), and answer the screen prompt *Copy What?* by tapping return four times to highlight all the blanks. Tap F8 and you will see *To Where?* Put the cursor on the first character to follow the moved material at the point marked B. Now tap F8 to complete the Copy. You should now have four lines of blanks on the form. Repeat the process by starting again at reference point A and you will have eight lines when you finish. Continue copying until your form is long enough (approximately 50 lines).

Save and exit the document by pressing F10.

Figure 10.3 – Before copying text

```
                    _____ <<
     <<
                         <->COMPUTER CENTER WORK LOG<<
  <<
  <<
  DATE IN    >>DATE OUT    >>DESCRIPTION OF THE JOB  >>OPERATOR NAME/SHIFT<<
  <<
  A_____    >>_____     >>_____      >>_____  <<
  <<
  _____    >>_____     >>_____      >>_____  <<
  <<
  B_____    >>_____     >>_____      >>_____  <<
  <<
  _____    >>_____     >>_____      >>_____  <<
  <<
  _____    >>_____     >>_____      >>_____  <<
  <<
  _____    >>_____     >>_____      >>_____  <<
  <<
  _____    >>_____     >>_____      >>_____  <<
  <<
  _____    >>_____     >>_____      >>_____  <<
  <<
  _____    >>_____     >>_____      >>_____  <<
  <<
  _____    >>_____     >>_____      >>_____  <<
  <<
  _____    >>_____     >>_____      >>_____  <<
  <<
  _____    >>_____     >>_____      >>_____  <<
  <<
  _____    >>_____     >>_____      >>_____  <<
  <<
  _____    >>_____     >>_____      >>_____  <<
  <<
                    _____ <<
```

Figure 10.4 – *After copying text*

USES OF THE COPY FUNCTION

There are many other uses for the Copy function. First, you don't have to retype information once you have already typed it. Second, you can also use the Copy function to duplicate material important enough to warrant a second copy. Copy can help you experiment. You can copy a paragraph or list, try out different ways of organizing it, and still have the original (possibly on a different page) if you decide you don't like any of your changes after all. Finally, you can use Copy to duplicate material that is needed in *almost* the same form. Copy your text to the new location and then make minor editing changes to it.

As you use and become more familiar with functions such as Move and Copy, you will find many occasions when you can use them.

THE EXTERNAL COPY FUNCTION

External Copy allows you to copy text from another document into the document you are currently working with. The original document is left intact, and the copied text is included in both documents.

Note: In the following example, *source* refers to the document or disk you are copying *from* and *target* refers to the document or disk you are copying *to*.

Start External Copy in the target document. To do this now create a new document called EXTCOPY. Put your cursor under the first character that will follow the new text you are bringing in. Since you are copying text onto the blank screen of a new document, the cursor will be located under the status and format lines.

Now press the External Copy key combination (shift-F8). You are asked to indicate the name of the source document. The name of the document is MOVE. Note that the drive location defaults to B.

If the source document were not on the same disk as the target document, you would type *A* after *DRIVE:* and insert the source disk into drive A. The prompt *Unable to Find Document* would remind you to insert the correct disk in drive A.

As the prompt instructs, *Press F10 to continue.* This action will move the cursor to the first character of the source document, MOVE. The prompt *START COPY WHERE?* appears in the upper corner of the screen. Place the cursor on the first character of the text you want to copy.

You could use a variety of means to move the cursor. For example, if the material you want copied starts on page 6, tap F1 and type 6 at the prompt *GO TO PAGE?,* and press return. You could use any of the cursor-moving methods covered in Chapter 3 to go to the beginning of the material you want copied. Just leave the cursor on the first character of MOVE. When the cursor is correctly placed, press shift-F8. The system prompts: *COPY WHAT?*

If you want the format line to be copied, press F9. Then highlight everything you want copied by pressing End and press shift-F8 again. After a few moments, everything you highlighted in the source document will be copied to the target document and placed prior to the point at which the cursor was located when you started the function.

USES OF THE EXTERNAL COPY FUNCTION

You can use External Copy to make back-up copies of documents using the procedure we just used for the document MOVE. You could also use External Copy to experiment with different formats or arrangements of material. This is particularly useful because the original document remains intact. You can also use this function to produce personalized form letters, envelopes, and single copies of merged letters (covered later in this book).

Press F10 to save and exit the document.

SUMMARY OF OPERATIONS COVERED IN THIS CHAPTER

Move

Note: F7 initiates and continues the process.

1. Put the cursor on the first character or symbol to be moved.

2. Press the Move function key (F7); *Move What?* appears on the screen.
3. Highlight the characters you want moved.
4. Press the Format key (F9) to move the format line along with the text.
5. Press the Move key (F7) again to indicate that everything is highlighted; the screen prompt *To Where?* appears.
6. Put the cursor on the first character to follow the material after it is moved.
7. Press the Move function key (F7) again to complete the operation.

Copy

Note: F8 initiates and continues the process.

1. Put the cursor on the first character to be copied.
2. Press the Copy function key; *Copy What?* appears on the screen.
3. Highlight the characters you want copied.
4. Press the Format key (F9) to copy the format line along with the text.
5. Press the Copy key (F8) again to indicate that everything is highlighted; the screen prompt *To Where?* appears.
6. Put the cursor on the first character to follow the material after it is copied.
7. Press the Copy function key (F8) again to complete the operation.

External Copy

Note: Shift-F8 initiates and continues the process.

1. Have the target document on the screen.

2. Locate the cursor on the first character to follow material being copied.
3. Press shift-F8.
4. Indicate the drive and name of the document you want to copy from.
5. Press F10 to continue; the cursor will move to page 1 of the document you are copying from, and the prompt *Start Copy Where?* appears.
6. Move the cursor to the beginning of the text to be copied.
7. Press shift-F8; the system will prompt *Copy What?*
8. Highlight everything you want copied.
9. Press F9 to have the format line copied along with the text.
10. Press shift-F8 again to complete the operation.

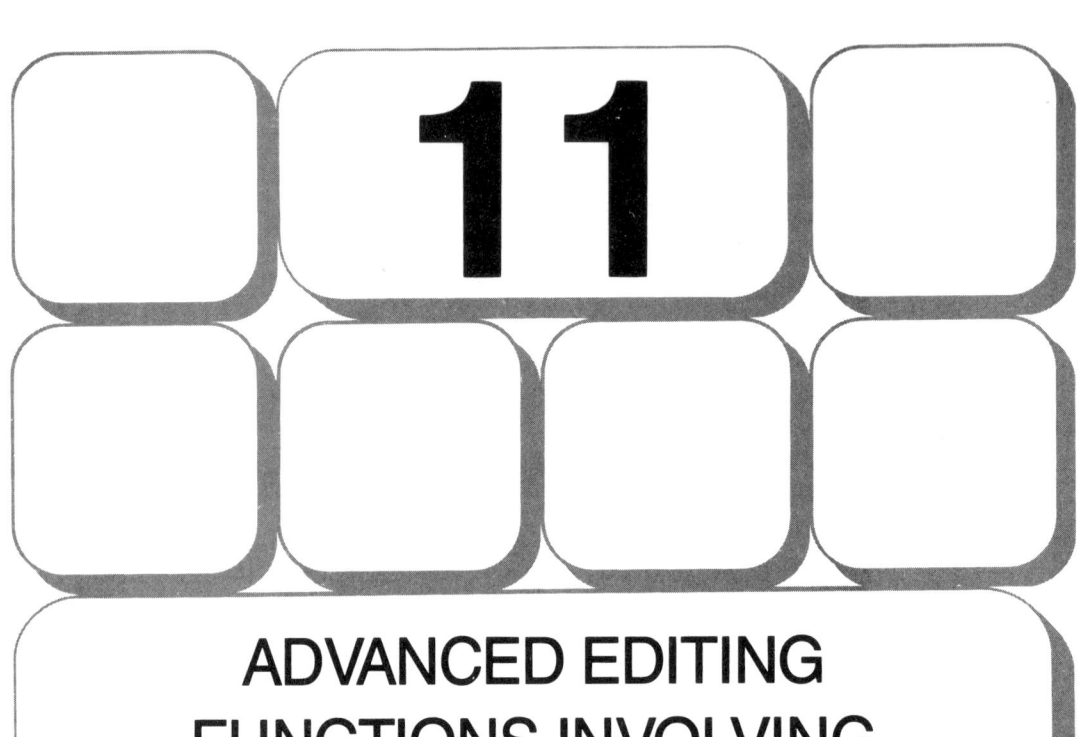

11

ADVANCED EDITING FUNCTIONS INVOLVING CHARACTER STRINGS: SEARCH AND REPLACE

You can use the MultiMate Search and Replace functions to find strings of characters and then replace them with other strings of characters. To try out the functions explained in this chapter, use the Edit an Old Document procedure now to put the document PRACTICE on your screen.

THE IMPORTANCE OF SPACES AND PUNCTUATION

In order to use Search and Replace correctly, you must remember that to a word processor, spaces, return symbols, tab symbols, and punctuation marks *are all characters*.

This can be tricky because we generally don't think of spaces as characters. For example, if you instruct the computer to search for the characters *me*, it will find all words that have *me* in them, such as "government," "mean," or "meet." But if you tell MultiMate to search for (sp)*me*(sp), you will find occurrences of only the word "me."

Punctuation poses another problem. In the above example, searching for (sp)*me*(sp) will not find occurrences of *me.*, or *me*,. So, you must specify only the space before the word, i.e., search for *(sp)me* to find "me," whether it is followed by a punctuation mark or not.

THE SEARCH FUNCTION

You can use Search to find a string of characters each time it occurs. You might want to Move, Copy, Edit, look it up in a dictionary or thesaurus, etc.

You could also use it to return you to a specific place in a document after you had to turn the system off or go to a different page temporarily. All you have to do is remember the last unique word you were working on and specify it in the Search.

You could also use Search to see how many times you have used a word. Maybe you think you may have used the word "basically" too much; you could check this with the Search function.

Search begins at the present cursor location and proceeds forward to the end of the document; the system will not search backwards. So to search the entire document, you must first move the cursor to the beginning of the document. (Use F1 Home to move the cursor there quickly.) Now press F6 to activate the Search function. The prompt *SEARCH MODE* appears in the upper right corner, and this line appears across the bottom of the screen:

SEARCH FOR: _____

The Search function allows you to specify up to 48 characters you want to find. That's many more than you usually need to use. Even the lengthy word "antidisestablishmentarianism" would be found immediately by searching for (sp)*antid* (as long as "antidote" and "antidepressant" weren't before it in the text).

The cursor is waiting for you to type the string of characters you want to find. So type in the word *efficient* now. Do not space before or after it. *Note:* If there were already a longer word on the line left over from another Search, you would use strikeover and Del to put only the new string of characters on the line.

The cursor will stop at both upper- and lowercase occurrences of your string of characters. This is called a *case blind* search because the system doesn't distinguish between upper- or lowercase. A case blind search for the string of characters (sp)*The*(sp) would find (sp)*THE*(sp) and (sp)*the*(sp) and, of course, (sp)*The*(sp).

You can also make the search *case significant.* This means the capitals will have to match your word exactly. To make the search case significant, press Alt-G after entering the group of characters you want to search for. *CASE* appears just left of the *S: N:* notation at the lower right side of the screen. If you want to do a case blind search later and see the word *CASE* still on the screen, you will have to toggle *CASE* off by pressing Alt-G. Tap F6 now to begin the case blind search.

After MultiMate has found the string of characters, you have several choices. You can:

- continue the search to locate the next occurrence of the string of characters by pressing F6;

- edit or delete the characters, which will stop the search (to continue the search again, press F6 twice);

- exit the Search function by pressing one of the cursor-moving keys. (If you press Esc, you will see the prompt *Do you wish to escape without saving this page? Y/N* at the bottom of the screen. If you pressed N, you would also stop the Search, but this would take longer than just pressing a cursor-moving key.)

After each occurrence of *efficient* is found, press F6 to continue.

You know the Search has been completed when the cursor is at the end of the document. If MultiMate can't find your group of characters, the cursor goes to the end of the document. You will see no screen prompt telling you that your characters were not found.

Leave the document, PRACTICE, on the screen for now.

THE REPLACE FUNCTION

Replace goes one step further than Search: it allows you to change the string of characters you find. As in Search, Replace allows you to specify up to 48 characters, it begins at the present cursor location, and it can be case significant or case blind.

You can use Replace to update documents. For example, let's say Morton Industries was renamed Mansfield Morton, Inc. and the company president became Norton Morton instead of Manfred Mansfield. You could easily do a global replace of the names.

Or, if you discover that Roger Smith is spelled Rodger Smythe, you can change the spelling quickly with the Replace function.

Finally, you can use Replace to fill out a lengthy repeated phrase. For example, instead of typing *word processing* several times in your report, type *wp*. When you are finished, use a global Replace to substitute the spelled out string, *word processing,* for every occurrence of *wp*. You can try this now in the document *PRACTICE*.

Press F1 Home to place the cursor at the beginning of the document once again, and press shift-F6 to begin the Replace function. You will notice the screen prompt *REPLACE MODE* in the upper right hand corner and the following information at the bottom of the screen:

TYPE OF REPLACE: 1) GLOBAL 2) DISCRETIONARY 3) ABORT

If you choose GLOBAL, every occurrence of the string of characters throughout the document will be replaced automatically.

If you choose DISCRETIONARY, the system will move the cursor to each occurrence and ask you to indicate whether you want it replaced or not. Press 2 now to choose DISCRETIONARY. This line appears at the bottom of the screen:

REPLACE WHAT? _____

Type *wp* and press shift-F6. The line at the bottom of the screen then shows:

REPLACE WITH? _____

Now type *word processing* without a space after it (in case a punctuation mark should occur after it in the document). Press shift-F6 and the cursor will stop on the first *wp* it finds.

The prompt at the bottom of the screen then says:

REPLACE? Y / N / ANY OTHER KEY TO ABORT

If you want this occurrence of your string of characters to be replaced, press Y; if you don't, press N. And if you want to stop the Search and Replace mode, press any other key.

Since this first *WP* is in a title consisting of words typed in uppercase letters, the *word processing* you have told the system to REPLACE WITH would be out of place. Press N to leave this first occurrence alone. When the cursor stops on other occurrences, press Y to replace all other occurrences of *wp* throughout the document.

It's safer to use discretionary Replace than global Replace. In either case, proof your document carefully! If you choose *Abort*, you will abandon the Replace. Now press F10 to save and exit the document.

DELETING WITH REPLACE

Here is another application of Search and Replace: you can automatically delete a repeated group of characters throughout a document. First, you would tell the system to search for the character string, and then after the *REPLACE WITH?* prompt, use the Del key to delete any characters which happen to be displayed. When the line is blank, press shift-F6 (or F6). This tells the system to replace the characters with nothing. Versions prior to the 3.2 update version do not have this capability.

FORMAT LINE REPLACE

The Replace function can also be used to replace existing format lines. This could be useful if you had several format lines in a document and you wanted to lengthen the writing line from 60 to 75 spaces to save paper and the cost of duplicating and distributing a report that is pages long. Here's how to replace a format line: locate the cursor where you want the Replace to begin. Press shift-F6 to

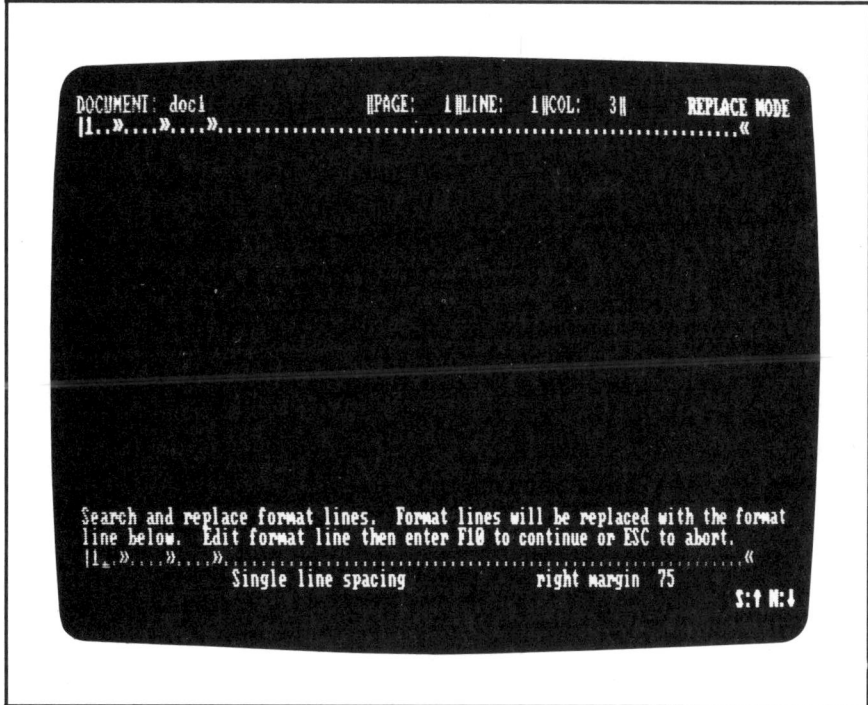

Figure 11.1 – Screen for searching and replacing a format line

begin the Replace function. Note the screen prompt REPLACE MODE at the upper right of the screen. Then choose either global, discretionary, or abort. The system will then ask REPLACE WHAT? You should indicate the type of format line replacement you want by indicating one of the following: shift-F9 (current format), Ctrl-F9 (system format), or Alt-F9 (page format). The screen duplicated in Figure 11.1 appears.

Modify the format line that appears, if necessary. Then press F10. If you chose to do a discretionary Replace, you'll need to press Y where you want the replacements to occur. Note: the format line above the cursor location is the one which will be replaced. To end the Replace before the entire document has been searched, press Esc.

SUMMARY OF OPERATIONS COVERED IN THIS CHAPTER

Searching for a String of Characters

Note: F6 initiates and continues the process.

1. Locate the cursor where the Search is to begin; press F6.
2. Press Alt-G for a case significant Search.
3. After the SEARCH FOR: prompt, type in the string of characters.
4. Press F6; the system will position the cursor at the first occurrence.
5. Press F6 to find next occurrence or edit the string of characters, which will end the Search.
6. Press F6 twice to resume searching after editing.
7. Press Esc to cancel out of the Search function before the process is complete.

Replacing a String of Characters

Note: Shift-F6 initiates and continues the process.

1. Place the cursor where the Replace is to begin; press shift-F6.
2. Indicate the type of Replace or abort.
3. After the *REPLACE WHAT:* prompt, type in the string of characters.
4. Press Alt-G to make the Search part case significant; press shift-F6.
5. After the *REPLACE WITH:* prompt, enter characters and press shift-F6.
6. If you chose a discretionary replace, the system will prompt *REPLACE? Y/N/ANY OTHER KEY TO ABORT* at each occurrence.
7. If you chose a global Replace, the Search and Replace occurs automatically and the cursor stops when finished at the end of the document.

Replacing a Format Line

Note: Shift-F6 initiates and continues the process.

1. Locate the cursor where the Replace is to begin; press shift-F6.
2. Indicate the type of Replace or choose abort.
3. After the *REPLACE WHAT:* prompt, type shift-F9, Ctrl-F9, or Alt-F9.
4. Modify the format line which appears on the screen; press F10.
5. If you chose to do a discretionary Replace, indicate *Y/N/ANY OTHER KEY TO ABORT* at each occurrence.
6. If you chose a global Replace, the Search and Replace will occur automatically and the cursor will stop at the end of the document.

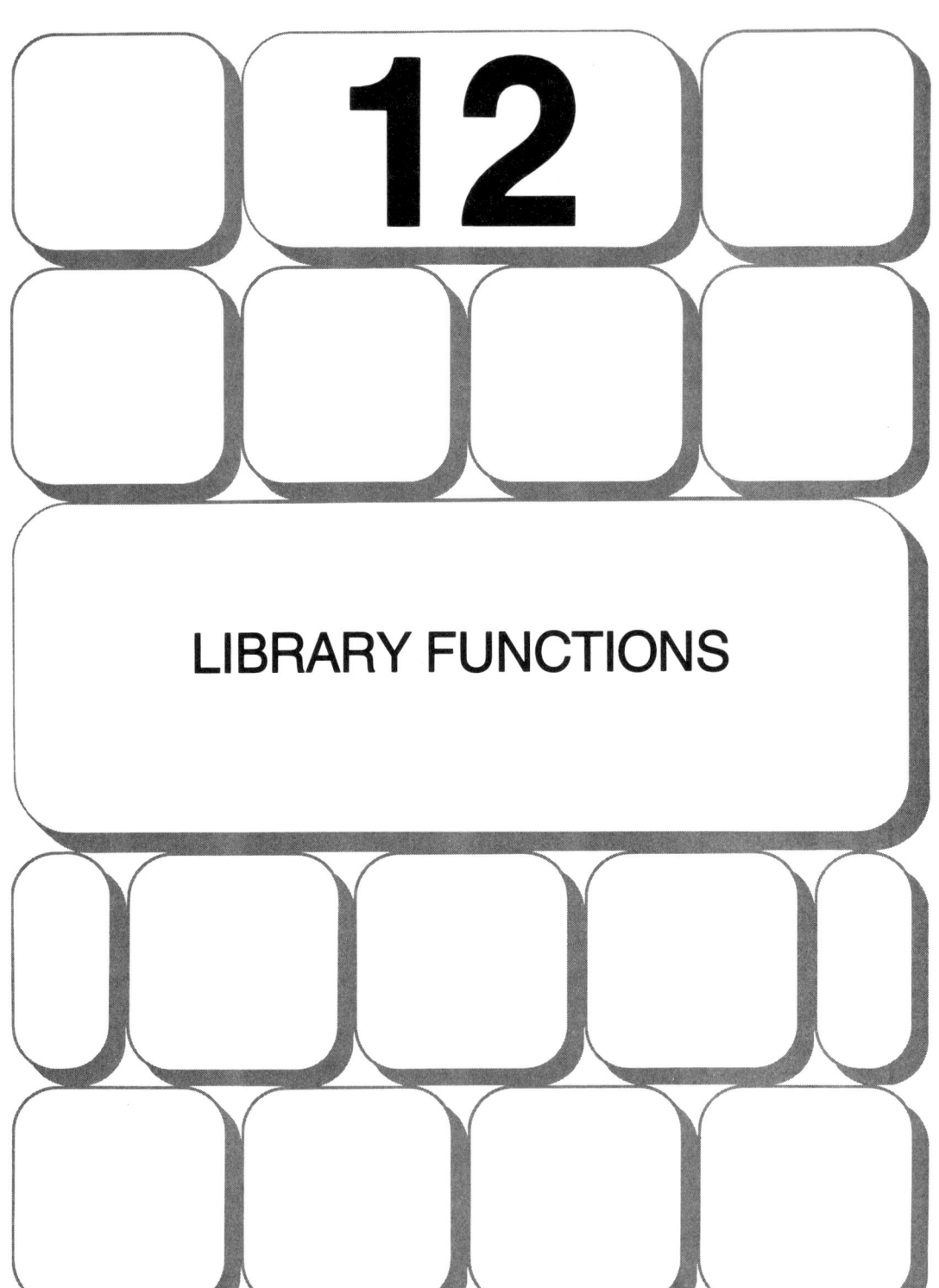

12

LIBRARY FUNCTIONS

The MultiMate Library function saves time. It enables you to type words, phrases, or formats once and recall them as many times as you need them throughout a document. You are able to recall even a lengthy paragraph with just one keystroke, which eliminates extra typing and error correction.

The Library function has three separate parts. You:

1. create a *Library document,* which contains the individual library entries or material you want to recall;
2. attach this Library document to the document in which you want to use it; and
3. recall individual entries from the Library document into your document.

Suppose you sell a product called the SUPER DUPER ELECTRONIC GADGET. Of course, you will want to use the product name frequently when you write sales letters to potential customers. Since this is a long name, it would be very helpful to be able to recall it with just one keystroke. You can use a Library document to do this. Here's how to set up the Library document you will use to type the letter presented later in this chapter.

CREATING A LIBRARY DOCUMENT

You create a Library document much the same way you create a regular document. Its name will appear in the drive directory, so you will be able to recall and edit it as you would any other document. This Library document can contain several *Library entries.* To create a Library document, begin at the Main Menu and use the *Create a New Document* option.

Now name your document. A Library document name can be up to 20 alphabetic or numeric characters long. Remember, only the first eight will appear in the drive directory, so at least one of these eight characters should distinguish it from other directory names. It is helpful to use *LIB* in the name of a Library document. Now type *LIB1* and press return to bring your cursor to the Document Summary Screen. Note at the bottom of this screen a flashing line says *If creating a Library, press F5 (Do not fill in screen).*

Since you *are* creating a Library document, press F5 immediately; don't fill in any items on the screen. At the bottom of a blank screen this line is then displayed:

Library Entry Name? [ ] Press shift F1 for a list of entries

You will usually include several entries in each Library document. Each will have a *recall name* by which you will call it into your document and each will be on a separate page. Because each entry will take a separate page, it can be up to 150 lines long (the maximum length of a MultiMate page). You could have up to 100 entries, but it would be difficult to remember recall names for that many.

The cursor is inside the brackets, which indicates that the system is waiting for you to name your first Library entry. Your recall name may be 1–3 alphabetic or numeric characters, in either upper- or lowercase.

For the name, use the first one or two letters of the words that will be recalled. For example, if you want to recall SUPER DUPER ELECTRONIC GADGET, give it a recall name of *S*. Also, if one of the Library entries is all lowercase and another is upper and lowercase, make the recall names reflect this. For example, wp = word processing and WP = Word Processing.

Use a name different from other Library entries in your document. *Note:* You can use the same recall name used in another Library document. If you can't remember all your recall names in a single Library document, press Help (shift-F1). This will show only names, not text, so if many entries have similar recall names, record them on paper. You may not use 999 as a Library entry name; it is used with the GO TO key (F1) to refer to the last Library entry.

For now, type *S* (recall name) and press return. A new screen appears, which is different from the one typically on the first screenload of a document. (Usually the status line says DOCUMENT and PAGE instead of LIBRARY and ENTRY.)

On this screen, the status line looks like this:

LIBRARY: LIB1 | |ENTRY: S | |LINE: 1| |COL: 1   1| |

Notice that *S* now appears at the top of the screen in the *Entry* slot, and your cursor moves to the first line of the Library entry screen.

Now type the exact words you want to recall: *SUPER DUPER ELECTRONIC GADGET.*

Note: Don't include spaces, returns, indents, etc. on a Library entry page unless you want them to be recalled every time. Also, don't put a space after the final character of a Library entry because you will want the cursor in the correct position to add a space, an s, a comma, or a period after the entry is recalled.

Now correct any errors with regular editing procedures. Then tap End to move the cursor to the last character on the screen in order to create a new page. Press F2 to make a page break and move your cursor to a new page.

You are ready to make a second Library entry in the Library document called LIB1. This second entry will be the word *information,* so type *i* for the recall name of your second Library entry and press return. The cursor moves to line 1 of the blank screen and waits for you to enter the characters you want to be recalled when you type this recall name. Now type *information.* Edit if necessary.

This was your last Library entry in this Library document, so rather than tap F2 (page break), you should tap F10 to return to the Main Menu.

You have finished creating your first Library document. *Note:* A Library document may not be printed out as a separate document.

ATTACHING A LIBRARY DOCUMENT

Let's use the Library document you just created. You will create a sales letter in which you will recall library entries from your Library document.

Create a new document named SALESLETTER and follow the screen prompts to get to the Document Summary screen. In the COMMENTS field, list the name of the library you wish to use, LIB1. Then, if you want to edit or add to the document later, you can attach the Library document and possibly eliminate repetitious typing. Now follow the screen prompts to the first page of the document.

Attach the Library document to this new document. Remember, only one Library document can be attached to a document at one time. If you tried to attach a second Library document, the first would be automatically detached as the the new one is attached.

When you are on the first page of the document, tap shift-F5 (the Library attaching keys). Notice the following line which appears at the bottom of the screen:

> What Library? Drive: B Name____ Press Shift F1 for directory

Enter *LIB1* (the name of the Library document you want to attach), and press return. The phrase *LIBRARY ATTACHMENT SUCCESSFUL* appears at the bottom of the screen. *Note:* You can follow this process when you are well into the document, and even when you are in Insert mode.

Your Library document is now attached to your new document, SALESLETTER. You are ready to recall the individual Library entries.

RECALLING LIBRARY ENTRIES

Type in the following document. When you come to one of the words or phrases that is in your Library document, press F5 (to activate the Library function), indicate the entry name, and press return. The Library entry is automatically displayed on the screen, and the cursor is in a position to continue typing.

After you type *SUBJECT:*(sp)(sp), stop and recall the first Library entry. Press F5. The following line appears at the bottom of the screen:

> Library Entry Name? [ ] — Press Shift F1 for a list of entries

The cursor is waiting inside the brackets for you to type the recall name of the entry. Type *S* and tap return. Continue typing to the next point at which you want to recall a Library entry. The next one will be *i* for *information.* Repeat these steps until the letter is finished.

> January 22, 19xx «
> «
> «
> «
> Mr. Jack Berglund «
> 1208 Cypress Lane «
> Seattle, WA 98003 «
> «
> Dear Mr. Berglund: «

≪
Subject: (S)≪
≪
Here is the (i) you requested on the (S). It includes an 18-page color booklet showing how compact yet sturdy the (S) is. Because it is available in four colors, one will surely harmonize with your existing system. ≪
≪
The best news is, of course, the price. The (S) costs at least 30 percent less than its nearest competition. ≪
≪
After you have had a chance to read the (i), give us a call at 555-9944 so we can set up a time for you to see the (S) in action. ≪
≪
Sincerely, ≪
≪
≪
≪
Amy Nelson, Sales Manager ≪
≪
Enclosure ≪

Press F10 to save the document and the Library.

Note: If you accidentally press shift-F5 instead of F5, you are signalling that you want to attach another Library document; the system will detach the Library document that you were using. So, when you then press F5, a screen prompt says *NO LIBRARY CURRENTLY ATTACHED.* This can be very puzzling. Just reattach the Library document with shift-F5 and proceed as usual.

When you save/exit SALESLETTER, the Library document is automatically detached. Both documents will then appear in the document directory. If you want to use your Library document in another document, attach it in the same way. You can edit an existing Library and add new entries as well. You can scroll through the pages of a Library document by pressing F1 (GoTo key) and then typing the recall name of the entry (e.g. *i* or *S*). Press Return and that entry page will then appear on the screen.

POSSIBLE ENTRIES IN A STANDARD LIBRARY DOCUMENT

If you type documents that are similar (e.g. mostly letters or reports about similar subjects), you could attach a standard Library document to each one. Following are examples of standard entries.

- current date: changes each day—include a Center instruction (if you want it centered) and include the returns which normally would follow it
- end of a letter: complimentary close, typed signature, title of sender, reference initials, enclosure notation, etc. (include all tabs and returns to put all of it in proper format)
- names of cities and states
- product names
- your company's name
- your company's address
- names and phone numbers of persons you might suggest the reader call
- any words or phrases you commonly use

Once you get used to using the Library function, you will come up with even more possibilities that are tailored to your situation and that will make your typing job easier.

SUMMARY OF OPERATIONS COVERED IN THIS CHAPTER

Creating a Library Document with Library Entries

1. Create a new document.
2. From the Document Summary Screen, press F5.
3. Name the Library entry (1-3 characters) and tap return.
4. Keyboard the characters of the Library entry.
5. Tap F2 to create a new page after each entry except the last.
6. Repeat the process for all Library entries.
7. When finished with the last one, tap F10 to save and exit.

Attaching a Library Document

1. From a page within a document, tap shift-F5.
2. Enter the Library document name and tap return.
3. *LIBRARY ATTACHMENT SUCCESSFUL* displays.

Recalling Library Entries

1. After the Library document has been attached, place the cursor where you want to add the recalled material. Press F5.
2. Enter the 1–3 character name of the Library entry. (Press shift-F1 if you need to see a list of the possibilities.)
3. Press return.

13

MERGE FUNCTIONS

The Merge function is one of the most common applications for which word-processing is used. You can use Merge to personalize a standard letter to send to many different people. The Merge function is valuable in business because an envelope addressed to *Mr. Jerry Perkins* instead of *Resident,* or a letter beginning with *Dear Mr. Perkins:* rather than *Dear Homeowner,* is more likely to attract Jerry Perkins' attention. It is also thought that personalized letters enhance a company's image.

To produce a personalized letter with the MultiMate Merge function, you create two documents which are combined or *merged* into one document when they are printed. The *merge document* or *primary document* contains the constant information that is the same for all recipients: the date, part of the salutation, paragraphs, formats, punctuation, etc. The *merge data file* or *secondary document* contains the individualizing information or *variables.* The variables could include the inside address, recipient's name in the salutation, appointment time, due dates, amounts due, etc.

When you print the two documents with the Merge Print utility, the system quickly shifts back and forth between primary and secondary documents, picks up the variables as they are needed and prints them in the appropriate places.

Although it doesn't matter which document you create first, let's try out the procedure now by starting with the primary document.

CREATING THE PRIMARY DOCUMENT

From the Main Menu, create a new document named PRIMARY1. Use PRI, P, LTR, or L, etc., in the document name to indicate that this is the primary document containing a letter that will be the same for all recipients. Follow the screen prompts to get to the first page of the document.

You will type *field names* that will be replaced by variables from the secondary document later. For example, the field name /-fn/- will be replaced by the recipient's first name when the final letter is printed.

Type the following material. Where you see the *merge code symbol* /-, press Alt-M (either upper- or lowercase). The /-ob/- stands for "omit if blank." Use /-ob/- after a field name if that field name might not be included in a file. For example, if the system does not find the field name called "title," it will simply omit the title and look for the next field name, *fn*. Type a space when you see (sp) so a space will appear between the variables when they are printed. *Note:* In this example *fn* = first name, *ln* = last name, *add* = address. (You can use any letters or numbers for the field names in your own work.)

```
January 12, 1985 «
«
«
«
«
/-title/-/-ob/-(sp)/-fn/-(sp)/-ln/- «
/-add/- «
«
Dear /-fn/-: «
«
Here is the catalog of Brown Bear products which you requested. «
«
We look forward to meeting your camping and outdoor gear needs.
Just call us collect, /-fn/-, if you have questions. «
«
Sincerely, «
«
«
«
Penny Anderson, Sales Manager «
«
Enclosure «
```

Now access the Create a New Document function directly from this document by pressing Alt-2 to begin the secondary document. You could also have pressed F10 (to save and exit to the Main Menu) and then created a new document.

CREATING THE SECONDARY DOCUMENT

Name this new document SECOND1. Again, it helps if you use SEC, S, VAR, V, etc., in the name to designate that it is a secondary document.

On the Modify Document Defaults screen, disable the automatic page break function by pressing N after that field. You should put a page break only after the last variable item for each letter. If you don't disable the function, a page break will automatically occur when you come to line 55 whether or not you have finished the whole set of variables.

Follow the screen prompts to page 1, and type the secondary document exactly as shown below. As before, press Alt-M to create the merge code symbol.

/-fn/-≪
Jerry/-≪
≪
/-ln/-≪
Holcomb/-≪
≪
/-add/-≪
1230 Pine Tree Road ≪
Goble, Oregon 78998/-≪
≪

Now press F2 to create a page break and keep all of the variables for a single letter on the same page. Type the next set of variables on page 2.

/-title/-≪
Ms./-≪
≪
/-fn/-≪
Jayn/-≪
≪
/-ln/-≪
Little/-≪
≪
/-add/-≪
8181 Opal Street ≪
Longview, WA 98632/-≪
≪

Don't put a page break after this last set of variables. The system assumes a page break will be followed by a page of variables. If it encounters a blank page, the Merge function won't work.

Although merge field names can be up to 12 alphabetic or numeric characters long, you will probably want to make them as short as possible since you may have to type them several times.

There are many ways to set up field names. Two ways are shown in Figure 13.1. Choose the correct method according to whether you anticipate using a first name independently of the last name (Example 2) or always using them together (Example 1).

In MultiMate, a secondary document can have a maximum of 75 fields per page and a maximum of 255 pages (sets of information for different individuals) per document. The merge fields can be in any order in the secondary document, and the same field (e.g. /-fn/-) could be used several times throughout the merge document. In the letter you just typed, *fn* appears three times, but it is listed only once in the secondary document. MultiMate searches through the entire page of the secondary document to find one field name that might occur many times in the primary document.

PRINTING THE MERGED DOCUMENTS

To print a merged document, access the Merge Print utility. There are two ways to do this.

1. From the Main Menu, choose option 5 and press return.
2. From a document page, press Alt-5.

```
            Example 1                          Example 2

    /-add/-<<                           /-fn/-<<
    Mrs. Marcia Henkle<<                Marcia/-<<
    2839 West Palace Street<<
    Wenatchee, WA   98883/-<<           /-ln/-<<
                                        Henkle/-<<

                                        /-add/-<<
                                        2839 West Palace Street<<
                                        Wenatchee, WA   98883/-<<
```

Figure 13.1 – *Two methods of setting up field names*

In this case, your secondary document is still on the screen, so press Alt-5. You will see the first screen of the Merge Print utility, as shown in Figure 13.2.

Now identify the two documents you want merged. The merge document is PRIMARY1 and the merge data file is SECOND1. Enter these names on the screen and press F10. The system displays the Submit a Document for Printing screen. This was explained in detail in Chapter 8. You can tab through the defaults and, if necessary, change them as directed in Chapter 8. *Note:* The items on this screen refer to the primary document only. For example, you can print part of the primary document (*Print from Page 001 and Print Through Page 001*), but you can not print just part of the secondary document. As we will see, you can use External Copy to print just a part of the secondary document.

The setting for *print in (B)ackground and (F)oreground?* should be left on *B*. All merge printing is automatically performed in foreground printing mode, so no change of this setting is necessary.

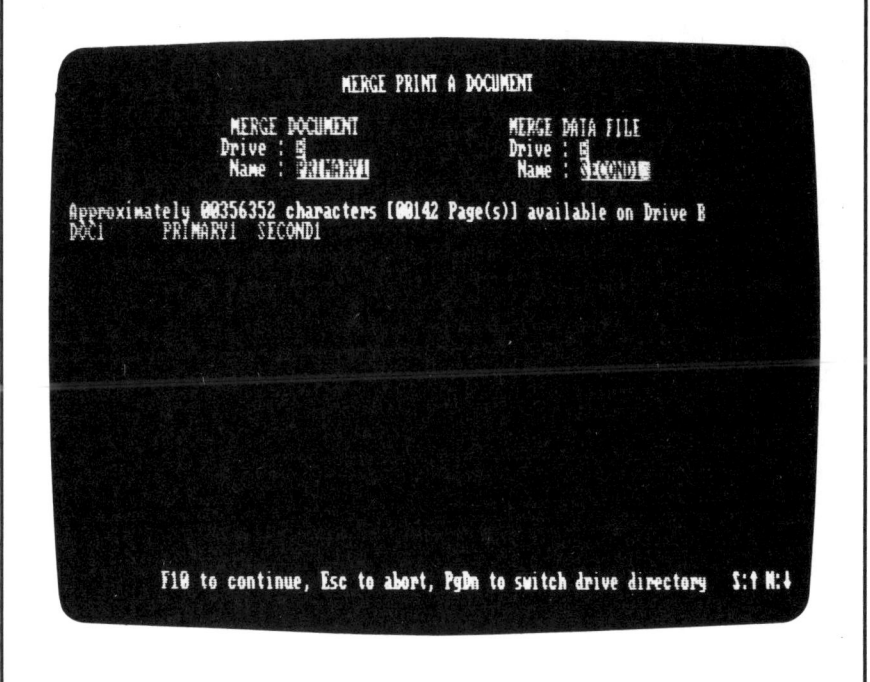

Figure 13.2 – Merge Print utility screen

This means that you can *not* work on another document during Merge Print.

When the settings on the Submit a Document for Printing screen are correct, the printer is on, and the paper is properly set up, press F10 to start printing.

The system prints everything in the primary document until it encounters a merge code symbol (/-) followed by a field name. Then, it switches to the first page of the secondary document and finds a merge code symbol followed by the same field name. For example, upon encountering /-fn/- in the primary document, the system switches to the secondary document and looks for the /-fn/- label.

Once found, it replaces the symbol with the correct information. The system then resumes printing the primary document until it finds another merge code symbol. This switching back and forth happens so rapidly that the system does not even pause. The recipient will see a letter which appears to have been individually created for him or her.

TROUBLESHOOTING WHEN THE MERGE FUNCTION DOESN'T WORK

The Merge function is fussy. If your merged letter doesn't print properly, try checking the following:

1. The merge symbol (created with Alt-M) must appear before and after field names in both documents.

2. A merge symbol must appear only after (not before and after) every variable item in the secondary document.

3. A merge symbol must be included after the last variable item in the secondary document.

4. No page break may follow the last variable item in the secondary document.

5. Merge field names must match exactly (right down to the spaces and use of upper- and lowercase letters).

There are lots of chances for you to goof when you use the Merge function; there is no substitute for proofreading with an eagle eye.

PRINTING ONLY ONE OF SEVERAL LETTERS

Let's say you are creating letters to four people and make errors in the third one. You don't have to print the first two again in order to get a corrected copy of the third. To redo just the third letter, create a new document and use External Copy (see Chapter 10) to copy the variables for the third letter from the secondary document into the new document. Then Merge Print the original primary document and the new secondary document containing only the one set of variables.

AN UNUSUAL SITUATION TO WATCH OUT FOR

If a variable that is an abbreviation followed by a period is the last item in a sentence, do not include the period in the variable. Doing so would put two periods at the end of the sentence. For example, your primary document might say, *Here is the information you requested about /-company/-.* If the secondary document says, */-Johnson Bros./-* you will get two periods at the end of the sentence. So, you must use */-Johnson Bros/-* as the variable and put the period only in the primary document.

CREATING ENVELOPES FROM THE SECONDARY DOCUMENT

You can address envelopes using the variables already typed in the secondary document called SECOND1. You would create a new primary document that calls for only those fields you want to appear on the envelopes. You must also change the left margin and paper length on the Submit a Document for Printing screen, and have the printer stop between pages so you can feed in a new envelope. Let's see how this is done.

From the Main Menu, create a new primary document named ENVELOPE. On page 1, indicate which fields from SECOND1 (the secondary document) you want to appear on the envelopes. Follow this example:

```
≪
/-title/-/-ob/-(sp)/-fn/-(sp)/-ln/-≪
/-add/-≪
```

This will cause the system to search through SECOND1 to find the first and last name and address on each page and to print these in the configuration you specify, that is, with a return after the last name. *Note:* If the set of variables includes a title, it would be used; otherwise, the title will be omitted.

Now access the Merge Print A Document screen directly from the document by pressing Alt-5 and fill in the document names. Type the document name *ENVELOPE* after the Merge Document notation and type the document name *SECOND1* after the Merge Data File notation. Press F10. On the Submit a Document for Printing screen, make the following changes appropriate for envelopes:

LEFT MARGIN: 58
PAUSE BETWEEN PAGES: Y
DOCUMENT PAGE LENGTH: 25

Load your envelopes and press F10 to start printing.

Insert a new envelope when the printer pauses between pages (unless you are using continuous form envelopes). If you are printing addresses on labels, adjust the left margin and paper length to fit the label size you are using.

In Chapter 17 you will learn how to create a mailing list from a variable list by using the Merge function and how to create your secondary document with a lot less work by using the Key Procedures function.

SUMMARY OF OPERATIONS COVERED IN THIS CHAPTER

1. Create the primary document which will contain the constant information.

2. Use Alt-M, field name, Alt-M for each variable item.

3. Create the secondary document which will contain the variable information.

4. Use Alt-M, field name, Alt-M, variable, Alt-M for each variable item. Put a page break after each set of variables except the last.
5. Access the Main Menu, choice 5: *Merge Print Utility* directly from the variable document by pressing Alt-5. The Merge Print a Document screen appears.
6. Identify the documents to be merged and press F10.
7. Fill in the Submit a Document for Printing screen appropriately.
8. Be sure the printer is ready.
9. Press F10.

14

AUTOMATIC HEADERS AND FOOTERS

Headers and *footers* are lines of information placed at either the top or bottom of a page. As you might guess, headers appear at the top of a page and footers at the bottom of a page. MultiMate enables you to create *automatic* headers and footers. Although they will not appear on each screen page, headers and footers will appear on each printed page of the document.

Items you might include in the header or footer position are page numbers, dates, document titles, document identification numbers, total number of pages in a document, or some combination of these.

Odd-numbered pages and even-numbered pages within the same document can have different information in the header or footer. For example, the even-numbered pages could have a date and page number, and the odd-numbered pages could have the document title and the page number. These are called *alternating headers* (or footers).

RULES FOR TYPING PAGE NUMBERS ON LONG DOCUMENTS

There are many different rules for typing page numbers in documents: the recommended style depends upon which secretarial reference manual, company handbook, typing book, or report style manual you use as a guide. Here are some examples of placement rules for page numbers:

1. On the first page, omit the page number if it is a header. A footer may also be omitted.

2. After the first page, place a header or page number at the right margin on line 4 from the top of the page. A triple space would then separate this page number from the following text. The text begins on line 7, which is one inch down from the top of the page.

3. After the first page, center a footer page number above a ½ inch (three lines) bottom margin. Stop typing text on approximately line 54 and place the footer information on

screen line 57. (Exact placements are affected by double vs. single spacing and by the "widows and orphans" rules.)

Since text ends on line 54, there will be a triple space (2 blank lines) after the text before the printed footer on line 57. Line 57 of the screen is line 63 of the printed page because of the six blank lines in the top margin.

PREPARING PRACTICE DOCUMENTS

You will have two multipage practice documents (one for headers and one for footers), so let's now duplicate PRACTICE twice by using External Copy.

Use the Create a New Document procedures to get to the first screen of a new document called FOOTERS. Use the External Copy procedure (which is summarized at the end of Chapter 10) to copy PRACTICE on drive B. Be sure to copy the format line and use F1 (GoTo) 999 then Ctrl-End after the *COPY WHAT?* prompt to highlight the entire document in the quickest way. Then press F10 to return to the Main Menu.

Repeat the procedure to create a new document named HEADERS. When finished, leave this document on the screen.

CREATING AUTOMATIC HEADERS

It is usually easier to set up an automatic header after you keyboard, edit, and paginate a document. Since page endings frequently change during editing, it could become necessary to relocate the lines used to set up the automatic headers if they are created too early in the process.

To set up an automatic header, place the cursor at the top of the first page on which it will be printed. This means your cursor should now be on the first character of page 2 of the document, HEADERS.

The format line above the lines which set up the automatic header determine the spacing, tabs, and line length of the header.

Use format change procedures now to change the format line at the top of page 2 so it will have single spacing and an additional tab at space 57. It should already have a 60-space writing line.

Because text has already been typed on this screen page, press Ins to insert the automatic header information at this location.

Note: Be sure there are no return symbols before the Header setup line. Press Alt-H (either upper- or lowercase); this is the header key combination. The header symbol (⊞) appears on the screen. Press return. You can then type up to five lines of information which you want to print in the header location. To set up a header that will automatically print on each page after the first the name *WP Report* and a page number which is preceded and followed by a hyphen, type the following line on the screen: *WP Report,* press tab twice, type hyphen # (that's shift-3) hyphen, and return. Press return two more times so the automatic header line will be followed by a triple space before the document text begins. End the header setup lines by again pressing the header key combination, Alt-H, then press return. Press Ins to toggle out of Insert mode. Now restore the document format line by pressing Alt-F9 and changing document spacing back to double spacing. Press F9 to toggle out of format mode.

Every printed page after page 1 will contain this header.

Figure 14.1 shows the top quarter of a screen with a header setup. Now press Alt-3 to access the Submit a Document for Printing screen without first returning to the Main Menu.

SPECIAL PRINT INSTRUCTIONS FOR AUTOMATIC HEADERS AND FOOTERS

Every Submit a Document for Printing screen has a line for headers and footers which says *Header/Footer first page number: 001.* This is where you indicate the first page number of a header or footer. In other words, if you want screen page number 2 (on which you put the automatic header setup lines) to be numbered as page 2, change the default to 002.

If you have not set up an automatic header or footer in the document, this line on the Submit a Document for Printing screen would be ignored by the system when it prints.

Check the defaults on the Submit a Document for Printing screen. Remember the document has a 60-space writing line. If you are

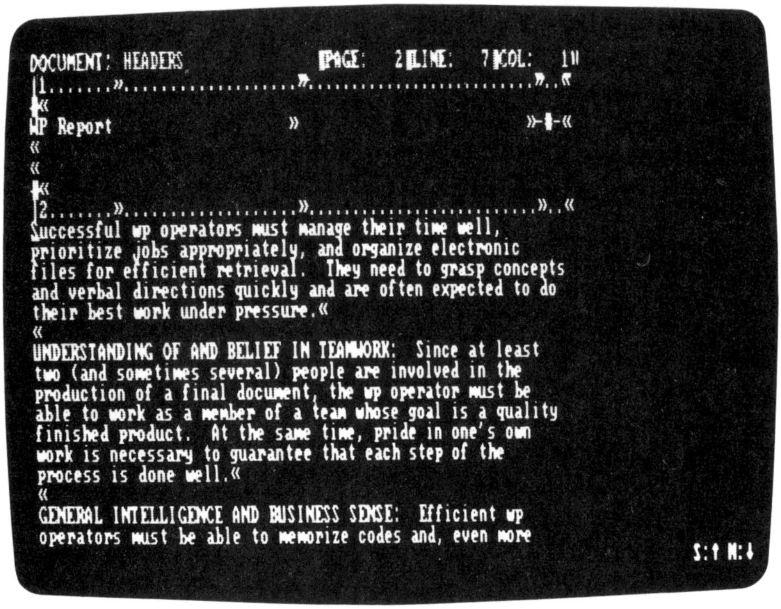

Figure 14.1 – An automatic header setup

using a printer with a pitch of 10 cpi, set the left margin at 010. If you are using a printer with a pitch of 12 cpi, set the left margin at 021. Set the top margin at 000. It will be easier for you to have the system pause between pages so you can roll the paper to the proper line (i.e. line 7 on page 1 and line 4 on all other pages). So set the *Pause between pages* default to yes. Press F10 when you are ready to have printing begin.

CREATING AUTOMATIC FOOTERS

From the Main Menu use Edit an Old Document to bring the first page of FOOTERS to the screen. Press Ctrl-End to move the cursor to the bottom of page 1. Then, since this page has fewer text lines than most will, put 8 or 9 returns after the text until the status line shows you are on line 56. Press the footer key combination (Alt-F) and return. Type the information you want to appear in the footer. Let's use a centered page number preceded and followed by a hyphen. First, press F3 to center the line. Then type hyphen, #, hyphen. Return after the footer information and end the footer setup lines with another Alt-F and a return. When the document is printed, the # will be replaced by an Arabic number.

Figure 14.2 shows you what the bottom quarter of a screen page with footer setup lines would look like.

PRINTING THE DOCUMENT CONTAINING AN AUTOMATIC FOOTER

Since the document, *FOOTERS,* is still on the screen, press Alt-3 to access the Submit a Document for Printing screen. The *Header/ footer first page number* line should be followed by 001 so the first

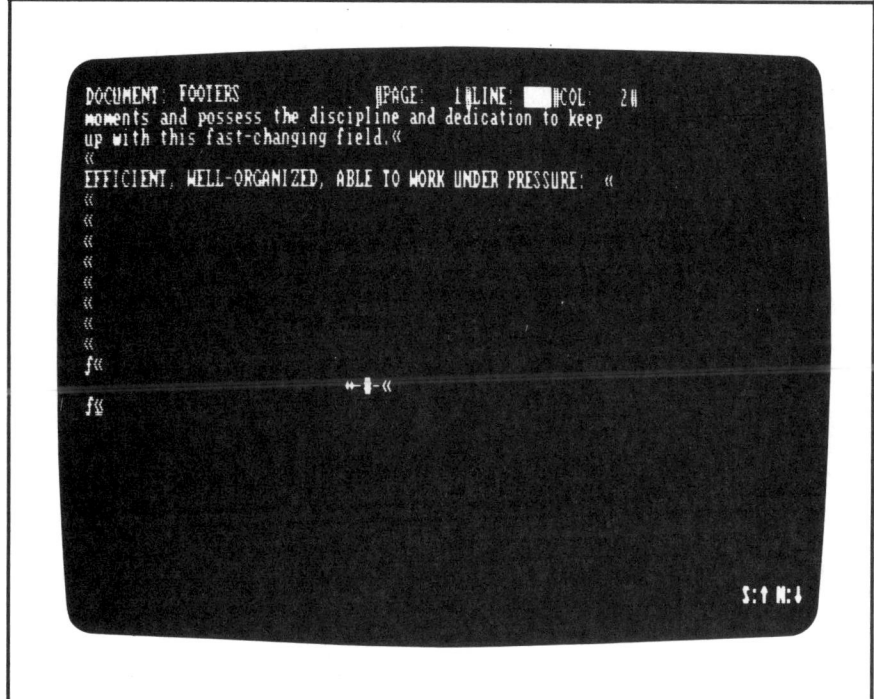

Figure 14.2 – A footer setup screen

footer will print on page 1. Change the top margin to 006 so the paper will automatically roll to the proper line. Set all other defaults the same as you did when you printed HEADERS. After the printer is turned on, press F10. A centered page number will print at the bottom of each page.

STOPPING A HEADER OR FOOTER FROM PRINTING

If you prefer to omit an automatic header on a page, e.g. the first page of a chapter, you can put a *null header* or empty header on the corresponding screen page.

A null header stops automatic headers from printing on all subsequent odd or even pages, depending upon which screen page the null header is on. To stop *all* automatic headers from printing, put a null header on *both* an odd and an even-numbered page. If you want automatic headers to begin printing again after you have used null headers, set up the automatic header on the screen pages again.

Here is the procedure for creating a null header: at the top of the screen "page" where you want the automatic header to stop printing, press Alt-H, return, Alt-H, and return again. The null header setup lines will look like this on screen:

≪
≪

Null footers work exactly the same way, but you put them at the bottom of the page, use the footer key combination, Alt-F, and see the screen symbol ƒ .

PROCEDURES FOR CREATING ALTERNATING HEADERS OR FOOTERS

If you want different headers or (footers) on every other page, you can create alternating headers (or footers). You set up one automatic header (or footer) for odd-numbered pages and another for even-numbered pages.

Here is an example of a footer from the odd-numbered page which will print the chapter and the page number so they end at the right margin. *Note:* This setup requires you to have a tab symbol in the format line where you want the C of *Chapter* to begin.

>ƒ ≪
>   ≫ ≫ ≫   ≫Chapter 1/#≪
>ƒ ≪

Here is an example of a footer for the even-numbered pages. It will print the document title and the page number at the left margin:

>ƒ ≪
>   THE WORD PROCESSING GUIDEBOOK/#≪
>ƒ ≪

When you want to stop alternating footers, use two null footers, one on an odd-numbered screen page and one on an even-numbered screen page.

HOW TO TYPE "PAGE X OUT OF FIFTEEN PAGES"

In some headers or footers, you must indicate the total number of pages of the document as well as the number of the current page.
Here is how to set this up:

>   ≪
>ƒ ≪
>   Page # of Fifteen Pages ≪
>ƒ ≪

MultiMate will replace the number sign (#) with a number corresponding to the number of each page.

USING ROMAN NUMERALS IN HEADERS AND FOOTERS

The number sign (#) in a header or footer will be replaced only with an Arabic number (1, 2, 3, etc.). To number pages of introductory parts of a document (preface, table of contents, etc.) with lowercase Roman numerals, you would type the whole footer on the last screen of each page. You can't use automatic footers to create Roman-numbered pages.

SUMMARY OF OPERATIONS COVERED IN THIS CHAPTER

Creating Automatic Headers

1. Type, edit, and paginate the document.
2. Put the cursor at the top of the first screen of the first page on which you want a header to be printed.
3. Change the format line to single spacing and add tab stops if necessary.
4. If text appears on this screen page, get into Insert mode by pressing Ins.
5. Press Alt-H; the header symbol (╫) appears.
6. Press return.
7. Type up to five lines which you want printed in the header position.
8. Press return three times.
9. To end the function, press Alt-H; the header symbol appears on the screen.
10. Restore the format line to double spacing for the document if necessary.

Creating Automatic Footers

1. Type, edit, and paginate the document.
2. Put the cursor at the bottom of the last screen of the first page on which you want a footer printed.
3. Press Alt-F; the footer symbol (f) appears.
4. Press return.
5. Type up to five lines which you want printed in the footer.
6. Press return.
7. To end the function, use Alt-F; the footer symbol appears on the screen.

Creating Alternating Automatic Headers and Footers

1. Follow the steps above for creating an automatic header (or footer) on an odd-numbered page.

2. Repeat the steps on an even numbered page with different information between the header (or footer) symbols.

Creating a Null Header or Footer

1. Follow the steps to create an automatic header or footer, but don't type anything between the header or footer symbols.

15

COLUMN MANIPULATION FUNCTIONS

In this chapter, you will learn to manipulate columnar text using four functions: Insert, Delete, Move, and Copy. These functions have three things in common:

1. You must use shift-F3 to get into Column mode before you can perform a column manipulation function.
2. Column mode functions cannot cross page breaks.
3. You abort a Column mode function by pressing Esc.

COLUMN INSERT

Let's first learn to insert characters into existing columns to make room for longer numbers (or text). Create a new document named COLUMNS and follow screen prompts to get to the first page of the document. Use format change techniques to set double spacing, new tabs only in columns 15 and 30, and a new writing line length of 35 columns.

Beginning at the left edge of the screen, type *123*. Then tab and type *712*. Tab again, type *324*, and return. Finish typing the table until it looks like this:

```
    123    ≫712   ≫324≪
    235    ≫434   ≫225≪
    556    ≫665   ≫932≪
```

Let's now insert three spaces before each of the numbers in the middle column. First, place the cursor on the first character to follow the insertion. In this case, that's the 7 of 712. *Note:* If you wanted to insert at the *end* of the number in the first column, you would place the cursor on the tab in the second column.

Access the Column mode by pressing shift-F3; you will see the prompt *COLUMN MODE* at the upper right of the screen. Press Ins to access Column Insert mode (you will see *COLUMN INSERT* at the upper right of the screen).

A prompt in the lower left of the screen asks you to *INSERT # of Columns 00 # of Lines 00*. Type the number of columns (spaces) you want inserted (03) and press return. Then indicate the number of lines (01 to 99) you want affected. Type *03,* and press F10 to complete the insert. The existing text moves right to accommodate the extra spaces as shown below. The newly added spaces are illustrated by # .

```
123   ≫###712   ≫324≪
235   ≫###434   ≫225≪
556   ≫###665   ≫932≪
```

Now change 712 to 87,712. You have room to do this and the numbers in the other lines of the column remain aligned because of the spaces you inserted. If you hadn't inserted the spaces with Column Insert, you would have had to go to the first number in each line of the second column and insert three spaces. Column Insert allows you to do this in one operation.

COLUMN DELETE

You can delete characters, including spaces, in consecutive lines of columns using Column Delete. In regular Delete mode, you must highlight the right hand side of a line before you can highlight any part of the line below it. As soon as you try to move down a line when you are highlighting in Delete mode, you highlight the entire line. In Column Delete, you highlight only the items in the column, not the whole line.

To try a Column Delete, use the table already on your screen; it looks like this:

```
123   ≫ 87,712   ≫324≪
235   ≫###434    ≫225≪
556   ≫###665    ≫932≪
```

Now delete the items in the second column which you just added. First, place the cursor in the top line on the first column you want to delete, in this case, on the *8.* Use shift-F3 to get in Column mode; the prompt, *COLUMN MODE,* will appear at the upper right of the screen.

While in Column mode, press Del; you will then see the prompt, *COLUMN DELETE,* at the upper right of the screen.

At the same time you will see this prompt at the bottom of the screen: <←> and <→> to Define Width THEN <↓> to Define Length.

Note: Once you start using the down cursor mover <↓>, you can't go back to using the left and right cursor movers to define column width differently. Also, once you use the down cursor mover, you can dehighlight only back up as far as one line below the line you originally started on. To abort the function, press Esc.

Press the right cursor mover twice to highlight the width of the column you want deleted and press the down cursor mover twice to highlight the length (vertical lines) you want deleted. When all is highlighted, press Del; your screen should look like this:

```
123    ≫712    ≫324≪
235    ≫434    ≫225≪
556    ≫665    ≫932≪
```

Note: If you were deleting an entire column, you would have to also highlight the tabs that begin the column. If you didn't, they will continue to "hold the place of" the deleted columns.

COLUMN MOVE

You can move a whole column of text all at once to another location on the same page. To learn how to move a column, use the three columns already on your screen.

Let's say that you want to reverse the positions of the middle and right columns.

With the cursor on the first character of the column you want to move (i.e. on the tab of the middle column), use shift-F3 to get into Column mode. Then press F7 to start Column Move. Note the screen prompts that accompany each step you take. Now it says *COLUMN MOVE*.

As in Column Delete, define the width of the column first with the left and right cursor movers. Press the right cursor mover three times now. Then use the down cursor movers to define the length of the column you want to move (pressed twice now). As before, once you use the down cursor mover, you can't go back to use the left and right cursor movers. Also, you may use the up cursor mover to dehighlight only up to the line below the original starting line. When the material you want to move (in this case, the middle column) is fully highlighted, press the Move function key, F7, again to make the function continue.

When the prompt TO WHERE? appears, put the cursor on the first character that will follow the column after it is moved. This will be the return symbol at the far right.

Note: The cursor automatically moved to the top of the column when TO WHERE? appeared. Since you cannot move across a page break, you sometimes may have to combine pages temporarily.

Push F7 to complete the move. Your text should look like this after the move.

    123   ≫324   ≫712≪
    235   ≫225   ≫434≪
    556   ≫932   ≫665≪

COLUMN COPY

Column Copy is almost exactly like Column Move; the difference is that after a Column Copy, the copied text will be in two places. On the example still on your screen, copy the second column so that it also appears on the far right of the screen.

To do this, use format change procedures to enter the format line, put a new tab at 50, and lengthen the writing line to 60 spaces. Begin the column copy by placing the cursor on the tab before *324*. Press shift-F3 to get into Column mode. Press F8 to access Column Copy. Now define your column width and length as you did in Column Move. When the column is highlighted, press F8, the Copy function key. To answer the prompt TO WHERE? use the right cursor mover and the up cursor mover to place the cursor under the return after *712*. Tap F8 again. *Note:* You must place the cursor under the first character to follow the copied material *in the top line*.

Your text will look like this:

    123   ≫324   ≫712   ≫324≪
    235   ≫225   ≫434   ≫225≪
    556   ≫932   ≫665   ≫932≪

When you have finished practicing the column manipulation functions, press F10 to save the document and return to the Main Menu.

Column Manipulation Functions 157

SUMMARY OF OPERATIONS COVERED IN THIS CHAPTER

Column Insert

1. Place the cursor on the horizontal column that will follow the inserted spaces.
2. Press shift-F3 to get into Column mode.
3. Press Ins to get into Column Insert mode.
4. Indicate *# of Columns 00 # of lines 00* with two digit numbers.
5. Press F10 to complete the insert.

Column Delete

1. Place the cursor at the top of a column you want to delete.
2. Press shift-F3 to get into Column mode.
3. Press Del to get into Column Delete mode.
4. Define the width of the column with the left and right cursor movers.
5. Define the column length with the down cursor mover.
6. After everything is highlighted, press Del.

Column Move

1. Place the cursor on the first line of the column you want moved.
2. Press shift-F3 to get into Column mode.
3. Press F7 to get into Column Move mode. *COLUMN MOVE* appears.
4. Define the width of the column with the left and right cursor movers.
5. Define the column length with the down cursor mover.

6. After everything is highlighted, press F7 to continue Column Move.
7. Prompt *TO WHERE?* appears.
8. Place the cursor on the first character that will follow the column after it is moved.
9. Press F7 once more to complete the move.

Column Copy

1. Place the cursor on the first line of the column you want to copy.
2. Press shift-F3 to get into Column mode.
3. Press F8 to get into Column Copy mode. *COLUMN COPY* appears.
4. Define the width of the column with the left and right cursor movers.
5. Define the column length with the down cursor mover.
6. After everything is highlighted, press F8 to continue Column Copy.
7. The prompt *TO WHERE?* appears.
8. Place the cursor on the first character in the top line that will follow the copied material.
9. Press F8 once more to complete the copy.

16

DOCUMENT HANDLING UTILITIES

So far, most of the functions e.g. Move, Copy, Delete, etc. covered in this book have manipulated parts of documents. Document Handling utilities perform the same functions (and others) on whole documents or, in some cases, on several documents at once.

To begin any function in this chapter, you must access the Document Handling Utilities Menu. To do this now, start with the Main Menu on the screen, press 6, and return. Press Alt-6 if you have a document on the screen; this will automatically save that document and display the Document Handling Utilities Menu (shown in Figure 16.1) on the screen.

THE COPY A DOCUMENT FUNCTION

From the Document Handling Utilities Menu, now press 1 and return to access the Copy a Document function. Your screen will display the information shown in Figure 16.2.

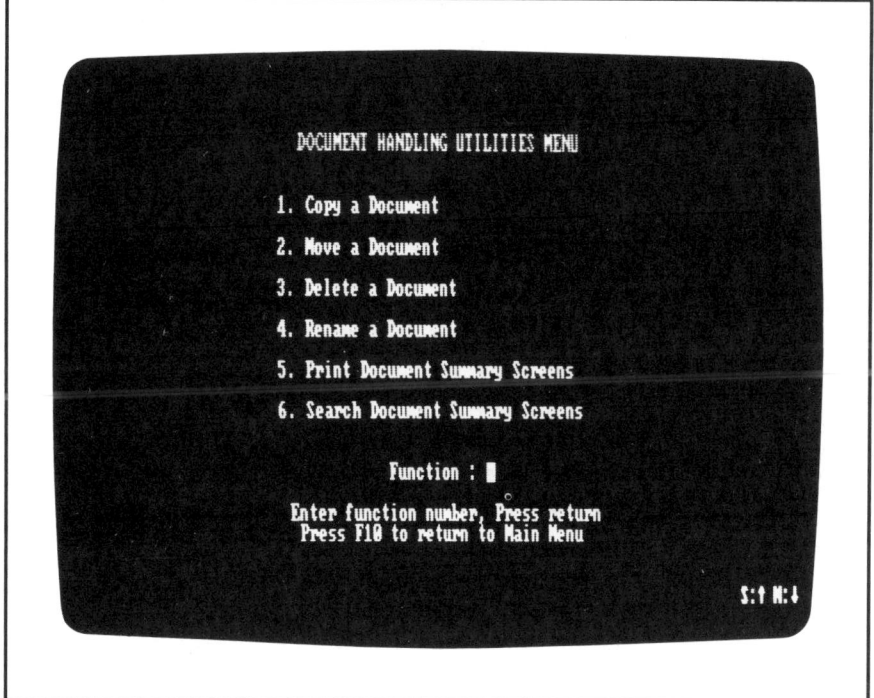

Figure 16.1 – The Document Handling Utilities Menu

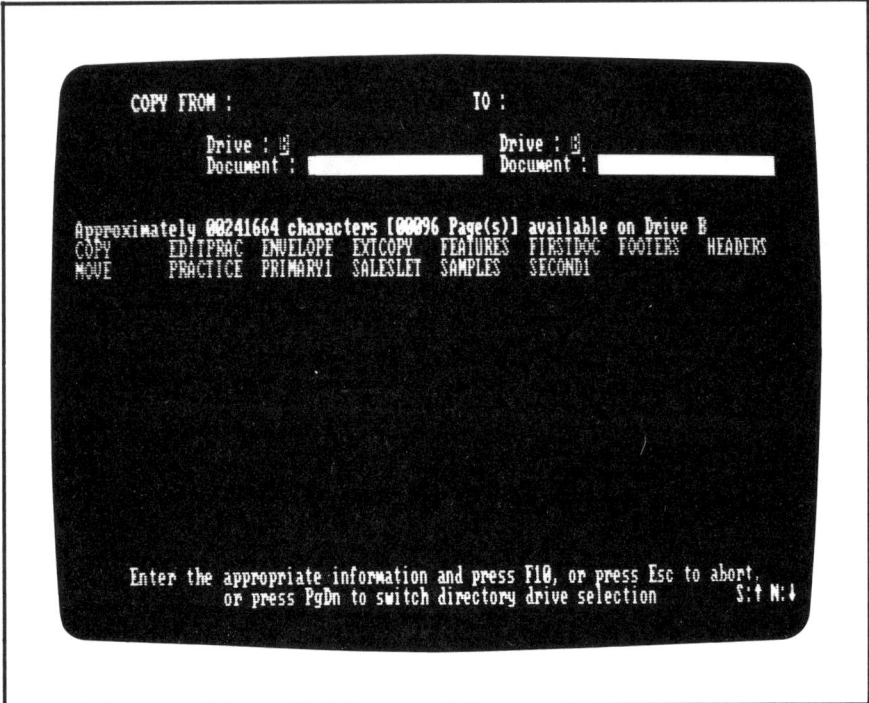

Figure 16.2 – The Copy a Document function screen

Note: You will not use Copy a Document to duplicate the document FEATURES on the same disk as the original.

The screen display shows a *From:* side which will be referred to as the *source,* and a *To:* side which will be referred to as the *target.* The default source drive is *B;* because the document you are copying is located on the disk in drive B.

Since the cursor is waiting for you to type in the name of the source document, type FEATURES and press return. The cursor moves to the default target drive notation, also a B. Since this is also the correct target drive, press return. *Note:* If you need to change these drive letters, use strikeover.

When you copy a document from one disk to another, the original and copy can have the same name. But, if you copy a document to the same disk, it can *not* have the same name. At least one of the first eight characters in the name must be different. The screen prompt: *A DOCUMENT MAY NOT BE MOVED/COPIED TO ITSELF* lets you know you must change at least one character of the name. The cursor is now waiting for you to enter the name of the target document, so type *2FEATURES.* Press F10. The screen says: *INSERT DISKETTE(S), STRIKE ANY KEY WHEN READY.* If the disks containing the source and target documents are not already in the correct drives, insert them now. *Note:* If you wanted to make a backup copy on a separate disk, you would remove the MultiMate system disk and insert the source disk (probably your document storage disk) in drive A and the backup target disk into drive B. At this point, you don't need to remove and reinsert any disks, so just press any key.

Once the process is in progress, the screen display reads: *OPERATION IN PROGRESS—DO NOT INTERRUPT—.* Finally, when you see *—OPERATION COMPLETE—REPLACE DISKETTES, STRIKE ANY KEY WHEN READY,* you know the document has been successfully copied. *Note:* If it were necessary, you would now replace the system disk in drive A and the document storage disk in drive B. Strike any key to bring back the Copy a Document function screen and then press Esc to get the Document Handling Utilities Menu back.

USES OF THE COPY A DOCUMENT FUNCTION

You should use the Copy a Document utility to create a backup copy of all important documents either on the same or different disk. The backup disks should be stored in a different place from the originals.

Copy a Document also enables you to make a copy of a document to experiment with. You can try different formats, paragraph sequences, or word combinations. If you don't like your changes, you still have the original intact.

THE MOVE A DOCUMENT FUNCTION

From the Document Handling Utilities Menu, type 2 and press return to access the Move a Document function. The screen will look like Figure 16.3.

As in the Copy a Document function, when you move a document, you must indicate the source and target drive letter and the source and target document name. The target document name does not have to be the same name as the source document name. This means you can rename a document as you are moving it.

Unlike Copy a Document, Move a Document requires two diskettes; you cannot have the same drive and document name specified after *TO:* and after *FROM:* If you do, the system will inform you: *A DOCUMENT MAY NOT BE MOVED/COPIED TO ITSELF.*

Since the source drive default, B, is correct and the cursor is waiting, type *EXTCOPY,* the name of the source document, and press return. Next, change the target drive to A and press return. Now type *EXTCOPY* again (in this example the target and source document names will be the same). Now press F10 to begin the process.

The screen will say *INSERT DISKETTE(S), STRIKE ANY KEY WHEN READY.* Your source and target diskettes are already in the correct

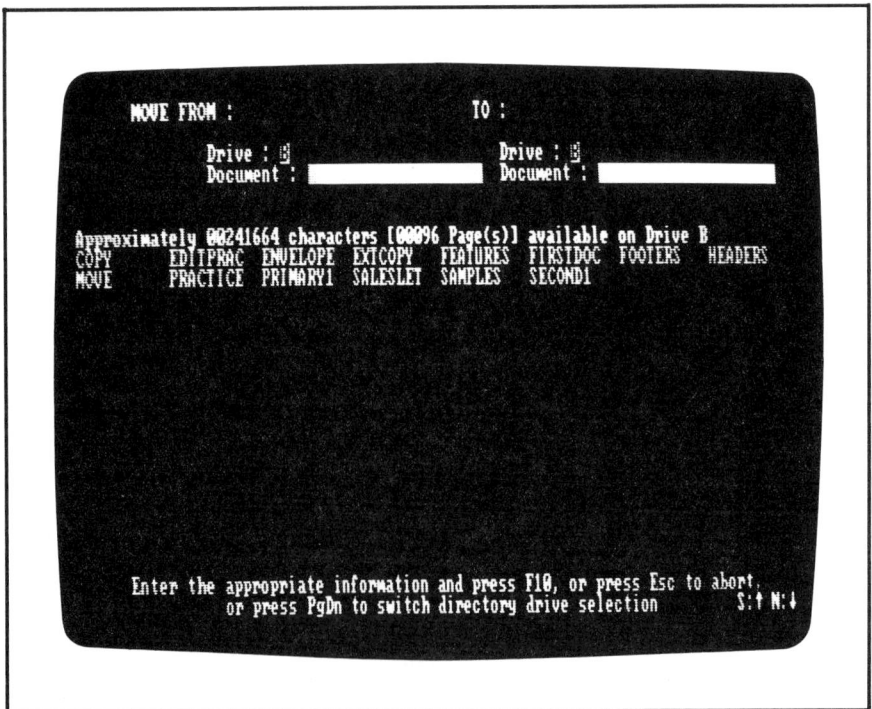

Figure 16.3 – *The Move a Document function screen*

drives because you are putting the document EXTCOPY on the MultiMate system disk that is in drive A. Then strike any key. *Note:* You could have put a formatted document storage disk in drive A instead.

Once the process has started, the screen reads: *OPERATION IN PROGRESS—DO NOT INTERRUPT—*. The document has been successfully moved when the screen reads *—OPERATION COMPLETE—REPLACE DISKETTES, STRIKE ANY KEY WHEN READY.* Strike any key to bring the Move a Document function screen back, then press Esc to display the Document Handling Utilities Menu.

USES OF THE MOVE A DOCUMENT FUNCTION

Move a Document relocates a document from one diskette to another. When you have finished, the document will no longer be on the original diskette.

You could use the Move a Document function to consolidate all documents of a certain kind on one disk. You could also move all documents by or to a specific person to the same disk rather than leaving them scattered over several disks.

THE DELETE A DOCUMENT FUNCTION

You access the Delete a Document function from the Document Handling Utilities Menu by typing 3 and pressing return. You will see the screen shown in Figure 16.4.

You must now specify the letter of the drive on which the document you want to delete is located and the name of the document. Since the document is not on the disk in the default drive, press PgDn to view the document names on the disk in the nondefault drive. To delete *EXTCOPY* from the MultiMate System disk, type *A* after *Drive:* and *EXTCOPY* after *Document:*.

Now press F10. The prompt tells you to: *INSERT DISKETTE(S), STRIKE ANY KEY WHEN READY.* The disk containing the document you want deleted is already in the specified drive so press any key.

When the process is in progress, the screen displays: *OPERATION IN PROGRESS—DO NOT INTERRUPT—*. Finally, when you see — *OPERATION COMPLETE— REPLACE DISKETTES, STRIKE ANY KEY WHEN READY,* the document has been deleted. Strike any key and press Esc to access the Document Handling Utilities Menu again.

USES OF THE DELETE A DOCUMENT FUNCTION

If you need to remove documents to create more space on a disk, use Delete a Document. *Note:* Delete a Document permanently erases documents from the disk, so be sure you have specified the correct document to delete.

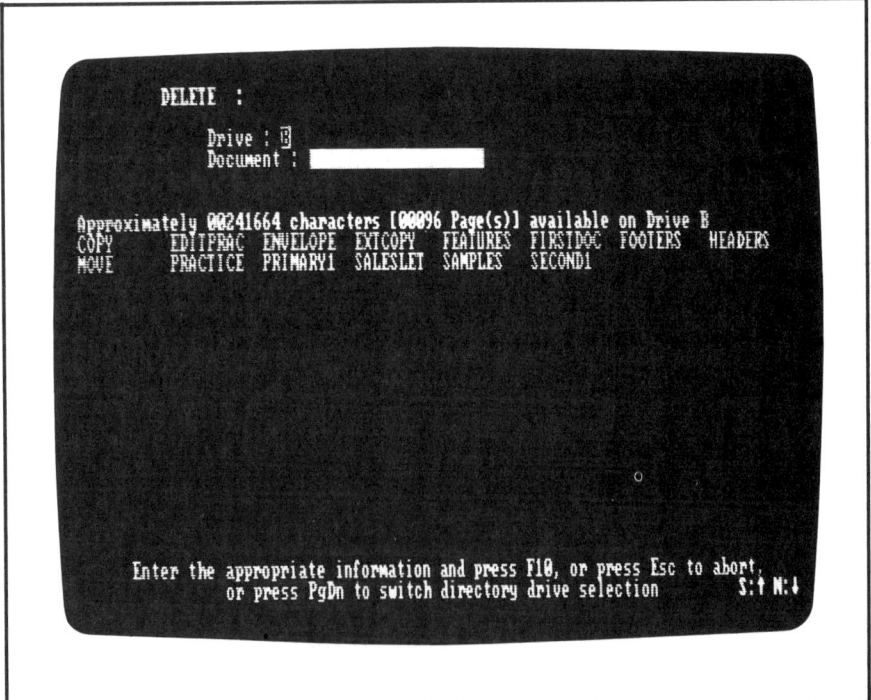

Figure 16.4 – Delete a Document function screen

THE RENAME A DOCUMENT FUNCTION

If you have created a document and its name is displayed in the document directory, you can change its name with the Rename a Document function. Sometimes you need to work with a document before the most appropriate name for it becomes apparent. With MultiMate, you have to name a document to create it, so you can just rename it later.

Now you will change the document named *2FEATURES* to *3FEATURES*. When the Document Handling Utilities Menu is on the screen press 4 and return. The next screen displayed looks like Figure 16.5.

Since the document is on the default drive, B, just enter the document name, *2FEATURES,* press return, and enter the new name, *3FEATURES.* Press F10 and you will see the prompt *INSERT DISKETTE(S), STRIKE ANY KEY WHEN READY.* The diskettes are inserted,

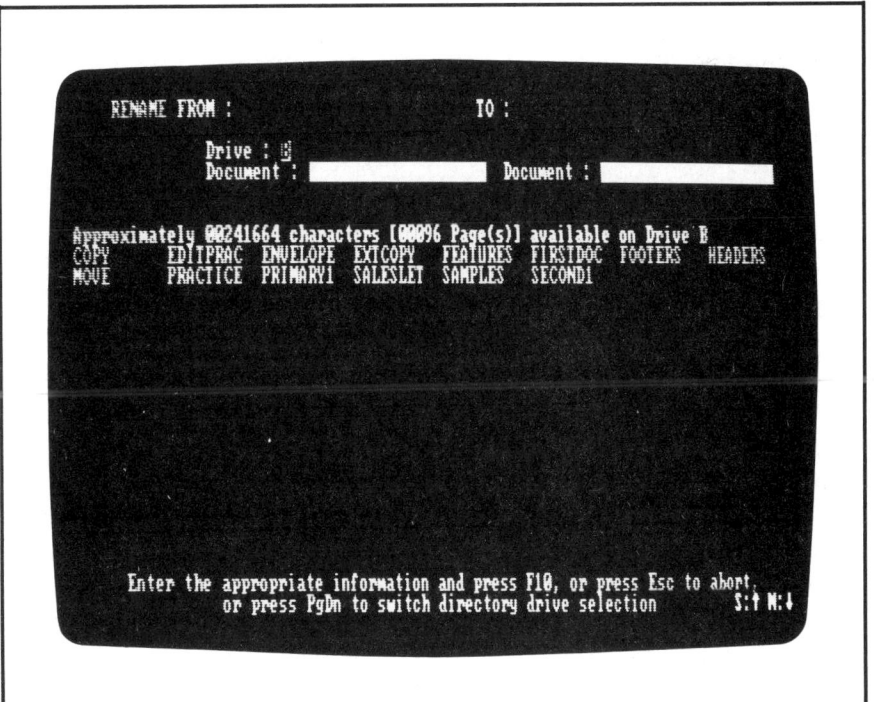

Figure 16.5 – Rename a Document function screen

so strike any key. You will see OPERATION IN PROGRESS—DO NOT INTERRUPT and finally, —OPERATION COMPLETE— REPLACE DISKETTES, STRIKE ANY KEY WHEN READY. Diskettes weren't removed, so press any key and then press Esc to get the Document Handling Utilities Menu back on screen.

THE PRINT DOCUMENT SUMMARY SCREENS FUNCTION

The Print Document Summary Screens and the Search Document Summary Screens (to be covered next) both involve the Document Summary Screens. As you know, that is the screen automatically created for each new document on which you can indicate author, addressee, operator, identification key words, comments, etc. You can choose to see the Document Summary Screens printed on the screen or on paper.

You might want to search the Document Summary Screens for all documents on the disk to find a particular document, or you might want to print hard copies of the Document Summary Screens to file reference information about the documents stored on a particular disk.

Press 5 and press return from the Document Handling Utilities Menu. You will then see the screen in Figure 16.6.

Since the default drive letter, *B,* is correct, advance by pressing tab, return, or the down cursor mover. Leave the default, *S,* (screen) to have the Document Summary Screens displayed on the screen. Press F10 to display the first Document Summary Screen. To continue to view the other Document Summary Screens, press any other key; to stop the operation, press Esc. After all Document Summary Screens have been displayed, the Document Handling Utilities Menu will return to the screen.

Note: If you want hard copies of all the Document Summary Screens, you must set *(S)creen or (P)rinter* to *P,* and turn the printer on *before* you press F10. They will print two to a page.

You will find this function most valuable if you always fill in the Document Summary Screens when you create or edit a document.

THE SEARCH DOCUMENT SUMMARY SCREEN FUNCTION

You can search through all the Document Summary Screens on a disk and get a list of those documents which have a specific characteristic. For example, if you have consistently filled in the *Author* and *Addressee* categories on the Document Summary Screen, you could search for all documents authored by Dan Volkmann or you could search for all documents addressed to Jane Patterson. Or, you can find a document which contains certain information you listed in the *Identification Key Words* section of the Document Summary Screen.

To begin this type of search from the Document Handling Utilities Menu, type 6 and press return. You will see the screen in Figure 16.7.

Be sure your printer is turned on and is ready to print. Press return to leave *B* after *Drive:*, designate *P* for *Printer,* and press F10

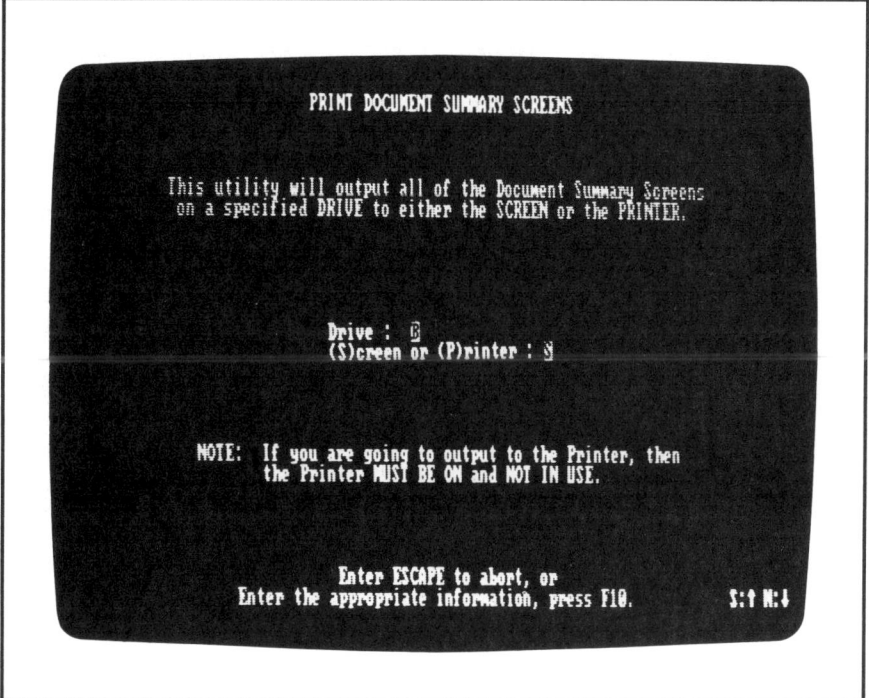

Figure 16.6 – Print Document Summary Screens

to continue. On the Document Summary Screen that appears, fill in whatever characteristic you want to search for. Use the tab, return, or down cursor mover to advance to the *Author* field, type *Carol Holcomb Dreger,* and press F10. The names of all documents with Carol Holcomb Dreger after *Author* will be printed.

You could also search for documents created during a certain time period. To do this, after the words *Creation Date,* specify *MM/DD/YY to MM/DD/YY.* Use two digit numbers with dividers to specify a beginning and ending date. The system will then print or display on screen a list of names of all documents created between those dates.

Use the category *Modification Date* in the same way to produce a list of the names of documents which were modified between any two specified dates.

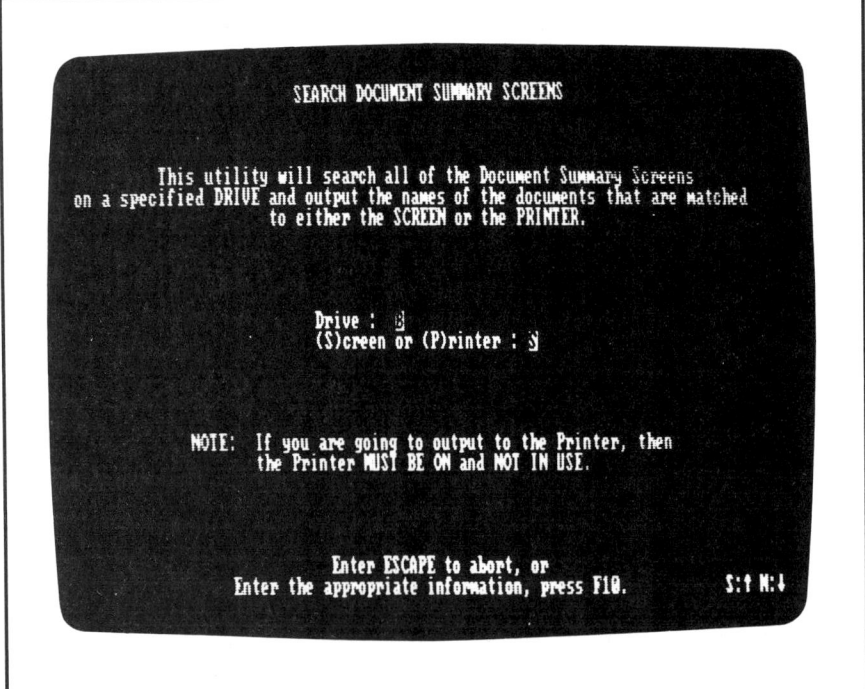

Figure 16.7 – Search Document Summary Screens

SUMMARY OF OPERATIONS COVERED IN THIS CHAPTER

Copy a Document

1. From the Main Menu, press 6 to access the Document Handling Utilities Menu.
2. Press 1 and return to access the Copy a Document function.
3. On the screen, indicate the source and target drives and documents; press F10.
4. Follow prompts about inserting or replacing disks to complete the operation.

Move a Document

1. From the Main Menu, press 6 and return to access the Document Handling Utilities Menu.
2. Press 2 and return to access the Move a Document function.
3. On the screen, indicate the source and target drives and documents; press F10.
4. Follow prompts about inserting or replacing disks to complete the operation.

Delete a Document

1. From the Main Menu, press 6 and return to access the Document Handling Utilities Menu.
2. Press 3 and return to access the Delete a Document function.
3. Indicate the drive location and name of the document to be deleted; press F10.
4. Follow prompts about inserting or replacing disks to complete the operation.

Rename a Document

1. From the Main Menu, press 6 to access the Document Handling Utilities Menu.
2. Press 4 and return to access the Rename a Document function.
3. Indicate the drive location and the old and new name of the document; press F10.
4. Follow prompts about inserting or replacing disks to complete the operation.

Print Document Summary Screens

1. From the Main Menu, press 6 to access the Document Handling Utilities Menu.
2. Press 5 and return to access the Print Document Summary Screens function.
3. Fill in the screen to indicate the drive and type of output, S (screen) or P (printer).
4. Be sure the printer is ready if you are printing a hard copy.
5. Press F10.

Search Document Summary Screens

1. From the Main Menu, press 6 and return to access the Document Handling Utilities Menu.
2. Press 6 and return to access the Search Document Summary Screens function.
3. Fill in the screen to indicate the drive and type of output.
4. If printing, be sure the printer is ready.
5. Press F10.
6. Fill in the Document Summary Screen fields.
7. Press F10.

17

KEY PROCEDURES

A *keystroke* is an individual stroke, tap, or depression of any key made while using a keyboard. Keystrokes include alphabetic and numeric characters, cursor-moving keystrokes, and even taps of the keys such as F2 (Page Break), F4 (Indent), and F9 (Format Change).

You use the Key Procedure function to save a great deal of time and typing. With it, you store *keystrokes* (combinations of typed characters plus commands) in a file so you can recall the file with a short name and *execute* (play out) the keystrokes as often as you want.

A Key Procedure file is somewhat like a Library document. However, the Library document is usually used for repeated words, phrases, or even longer text. A Key Procedure file is used for more sophisticated combinations of cursor-moving commands, functions, and words that you want to use repeatedly.

Here is an overview of the parts of the Key Procedure function:

- a. *Build:* You first build (create) a Key Procedure file. In this file, you enter all the keystrokes you want to be able to recall and have repeated. You can also build in two features: *pause* and *prompt.*

- b. *Pause:* Pause allows you to stop the execution of a Key Procedure file temporarily. You can then type information that will vary in each document, such as a name or a date. You plan the pause ahead of time and include it when you build the Key Procedure file.

- c. *Prompt:* You can choose to continue or stop playing back the Key Procedure file at predetermined points. When you build your Key Procedure file, you designate where (during playback) you want the option of deciding whether to stop or continue.

- d. *Execute:* Later, you execute (use) the file to play back all the keystrokes you built in.

Let's now see how these four features are combined to create a Key Procedure file.

BUILDING A KEY PROCEDURE FILE

The first step is building a Key Procedure file. From the Main Menu, create a new document named KEYPROC, and follow the screen prompts to the first screen of the document. This document can contain several Key Procedure files which will be used for different things. KEYPROC will be the document in which the system will find our specialty Key Procedure files when we call them each up by name.

Now press Ctrl-F5. Notice the screen prompt: *KEY PROCEDURE FILE NAME: (F10 TO CONTINUE, ESCAPE TO ABORT)*. The cursor is waiting for you to enter the file name in the blank area. *Note:* This file name should be 1–8 alphabetic or numeric characters long and should have no spaces in it. Let's name our first Key Procedure file CUSTINFO because it will be used to record information about new customers.

Press F10 to continue. The reverse video *B* appears on the *S: N:* line at the lower right of the screen until you toggle out of the build phase with Ctrl-F5. From this point on, *every* keystroke you type will be recorded as part of the Key Procedure file.

Let's begin by adapting the format line for this project. Press Format Change, F9, which places the cursor in the existing format line at the top of the screen. Spacing is already set on *1* for single spacing. Set tabs at columns 5, 15, and 35 only, and press return at column 58. To exit Format mode, press F9.

Now we'll set up the first category in which we want information and then a pause so the user can enter variable information. There is no limit to the number of pauses your Key Procedure file can have.

First, press tab to move the cursor to column 5. With Caps Lock on, type *NAME:* then tab. Press Ctrl-F6 to program in a pause. Press tab again to move to column 35. Type *PHONE:*(sp)(sp). Press Ctrl-F6 for a pause. Now you have set up headings followed by pauses to allow the user to type in a name and a phone number.

Note: You would, of course, put a prompt after the last item of information you intend to collect for a customer. However, you might also want to stop before going through all of the items. This would be appropriate if you had only a name and phone number for some customers and did not yet have their addresses.

Press return twice now to move down two lines and press Ctrl-F7 to add a prompt just in case you want to stop executing the Key Procedure file after the phone number.

Tab once and type *ADDRESS:*, tab, then Ctrl-F6 for a pause. Press return once and tab twice. Next, program another pause with Ctrl-F6. Now return twice, tab once, type *ACCT. NUMBER:* and space twice. Then program a pause with Ctrl-F6. Now press Ctrl-F7 to include a prompt so you can stop or continue to record information for a different customer. Then press F2 (Page Break).

Now stop building the Key Procedure file by pressing Ctrl-F5 again. The reverse video *B* between *S: N:* will disappear. Figure 17.1 illustrates the finished file. Press F10 to save the document and return the Main Menu to the screen.

EXECUTING A KEY PROCEDURE FILE

Before you begin to execute a Key Procedure file, you must place the cursor at the point in the document where you want the function to start. We will use our Key Procedure in a new document that could be printed on 3 by 5-inch labels. Create a document called FONEFILE. Then follow the screen prompts to get to the first screen of the document.

Now execute the Key Procedure file by pressing Ctrl-F8. *Key Procedure FILE NAME: (F10 TO CONTINUE, ESCAPE TO ABORT)*

```
        >>NAME:       >>            >>PHONE:    <<
<<
        >>ADDRESS:                  ><<
        >>           ><<
<<
        >>ACCT. NUMBER:
```

Figure 17.1 – *The finished Key Procedure file*

appears and the screen waits for you to enter the name *CUSTINFO* in upper- or lowercase. (If you just built it, it may already appear in the blank.) Press F10 to enter the execute phase. An *E* (execute) appears between the *S: N:* on the screen. The file will play back until it encounters a pause or a prompt.

Note: If you had named a file that doesn't exist, the screen would have said *FILE NOT FOUND, HIT ANY KEY TO CONTINUE.* At this point, you could try a different name. If that doesn't work, you should see if the correct disk is in the document storage disk drive.

Your Key Procedure file will execute from the format line change through the word *NAME:* and the tab.

Since you have put pauses in your document, this screen prompt should now display: *PRESS (C) TO CONTINUE. PLEASE ENTER DATA, THEN CTRL-F6 TO RESUME.* Press C, then enter your name as the first customer, and resume by pressing Ctrl-F6.

At every pause after the first, this message quickly displays and then disappears: *PLEASE ENTER DATA THEN CTRL-F6 TO RESUME.* After the word, *PHONE:,* and all the rest, enter information appropriate for yourself and then continue by pressing Ctrl-F6.

When a prompt is reached, this message displays: *DO YOU WISH TO CONTINUE OR STOP? (C/S).* Press C to continue. (S stands for stop.) Use the Key Procedure file one more time. This time, enter information for your best friend.

After the Key Procedure file has executed a second time and you have entered information in each category for your friend, your cursor will be at the bottom of page 2 waiting for you to type C or S. Type *S* (stop). The reverse video *E* will then no longer be displayed. *Note:* You could now continue typing the rest of your document as if this Key Procedure were only a part of it.

EDITING A KEY PROCEDURE FILE

Remember, *every* keystroke you make while building a Key Procedure file will be included in the file and will, therefore, be executed. Even if you make an error and backspace to correct it, *all* those strokes will be in the Key Procedure file.

You cannot edit a Key Procedure file in the same way you usually edit old documents because every keystroke in a Key Procedure file executes—even the original mistakes, backspaces, and revisions.

If you want to make changes in an existing Key Procedure file, you would have to write over it completely by using the following procedure.

Put the cursor in any document. Press Ctrl-F5 (the build combination). The screen displays this message: *KEY PROCEDURE FILE NAME: (F10 TO CONTINUE, ESCAPE TO ABORT).* Type the name of the existing Key Procedure file you want to write over, then press F10. The screen displays this message: *FILE ALREADY EXISTS—DO YOU WISH TO REPLACE CONTENTS OF THE FILE? ;(Y/N).*

Since you *do* want to change the file, press Y. (N would return you to your regular document immediately.) Type the keystrokes you now want in the Key Procedure file; use the same techniques you used before in the build phase. After you finish writing over the Key Procedure file, toggle out of the build phase once again with Ctrl-F5. If you made errors in your Key Procedure, correct them now with these techniques. Press F10 to save the document and return to the Main Menu.

Key Procedures is a very powerful feature that sets MultiMate apart from most other word processing programs. It can save you a great deal of time because it eliminates repetitive typing of frequently used text or formats. Be on the lookout for situations in which you can use Key Procedures. For example, you might use it for a memorandum heading with pauses after the *TO, DATE,* and *SUBJECT,* or for all the headings in a balance sheet format such as *Fixed Assets, Current Assets,* etc. with pauses after each for you to type in the current numbers. The possibilities are limited only by your imagination!

SUMMARY OF OPERATIONS COVERED IN THIS CHAPTER

Building a Key Procedure File

1. Create a new document that will contain your Key Procedure files, and follow the prompts to the first screen page.
2. Press Ctrl-F5 to begin the building phase.

3. Name the Key Procedure and press F10; a reverse video *B* displays between the *S: N:*.

4. Enter the keystrokes you want to be able to recall.

5. Enter a pause by pressing Ctrl-F6.

6. Enter a prompt by pressing Ctrl-F7.

7. Stop building the Key Procedure file by pressing Ctrl-F5.

Editing a Key Procedure File

1. With the cursor in any document, press Ctrl-F5 and type in the name of the Key Procedure you want to edit. Press F10.

2. In response to the prompt: *FILE ALREADY EXISTS—DO YOU WISH TO REPLACE CONTENTS OF THE FILE (Y/N)*, type a *Y*.

3. Redo the keystrokes in the file using the same techniques you used when you first built it. Press Ctrl-F5 to end the rebuilding phase.

Executing a Key Procedure File

1. From within the document in which you want to use a Key Procedure file, press Ctrl-F8.

2. Type the name of the Key Procedure file in response to the prompt and press F10.

3. The Key Procedure file will play out all characters, commmands, and pauses until it encounters a prompt.

4. Type *S* in response to a prompt when you want to stop the file from executing.

18

USING THE SPELL CHECK AND SPELL EDIT FUNCTIONS

Two new features of the 3.20 update version of MultiMate are Spell Check and Spell Edit, which enable you to verify and correct spelling. With MultiMate Spell Check you receive a *dictionary disk*. It contains 80,000 words and also a *Custom Dictionary* which you develop by adding words of your choice.

CAPABILITIES OF THE SPELL CHECK FUNCTION

The Spell Check function compares each of the words in your document to the words on the dictionary disk, then marks on the screen the words not found. You can then use Spell Edit to correct the words that are wrong.

Since the Spell Check function marks words as errors when they aren't found on the dictionary disk, the following, though correct, probably would be marked as errors:

- technical words or jargon peculiar to your field
- characters such as *2.* or *b.* that begin lists.
- proper names (unless they can also be used in contexts where they are not proper names, e.g. carol, don, penny, opal, etc.)
- words that contain a hard hyphen to divide them at the end of a line

There are other limitations. The Spell Check function will not mark words that are correctly spelled, but incorrectly used; for example, "I red the report last knight," or "I except you invitation."

It doesn't matter if words are capitalized at the beginning, all uppercase, underscored, or some combination of these; if they are on the dictionary disk, they are considered correctly spelled. There are also some inconsistencies; for example, some Latin terms are not on the dictionary disk (ibid. and et al.), but others are (status quo).

AFTER SPELL CHECK—WHAT THEN?

After it has completed its task, the Spell Check program informs you that it has found *[xxxxx] MISSPELLED WORDS [xxxxx] WORDS*

TOTAL. You then need to Spell Edit the document to correct the errors. The Spell Edit process also allows you to add words to the Custom Dictionary on the dictionary disk. You might want to include words that are not in the preprogrammed dictionary so they won't be considered errors the next time they are encountered in a Spell Check. This feature is limited by the size of the dictionary disk. That shouldn't be too much of a problem, however, since you should have room on the disk to add approximately 5000 words.

Note: Be careful when you add a word to the dictionary disk; if it's wrong, it will haunt you. For example, if you accidentally put *freind* in the Custom Dictionary, this incorrect spelling will not be marked as an error from then on.

Let's now try the procedures for Spell Check. If you are not sure there are errors in the document *PRACTICE,* use the Edit an Old Document procedure now to put in two or three errors. You may leave the document on the screen.

HOW TO SPELL CHECK AN ENTIRE DOCUMENT

The purpose of a Spell Check is to mark those words which are not found in either the original 80,000 word dictionary or your custom dictionary. To Spell Check the entire document, *PRACTICE,* access function 8 on the Main Menu in one of two ways.

If the document is already on the screen, press Alt-8. If the Main Menu is on the screen, press 8 and return. Figure 18.1 shows the screen which appears.

Enter the letter of the drive containing your document storage disk. Then type in the name of the document you want to Spell Check, *PRACTICE,* if it doesn't already appear after *Document.* Press return.

The screen now displays START PAGE [1] END PAGE [999] immediately under the document name. Since you want to Spell Check the entire three-page document, PRACTICE, leave these defaults.

Note: If you had just added some new pages to a document, for example, pages 4, 5, and 6, you could indicate START PAGE [4] END PAGE [6]. Then only the new pages would be Spell Checked. Use the cursor-moving keys to get from bracket to bracket, and use strikeover to change the numbers.

Using the Spell Check and Spell Edit Functions **185**

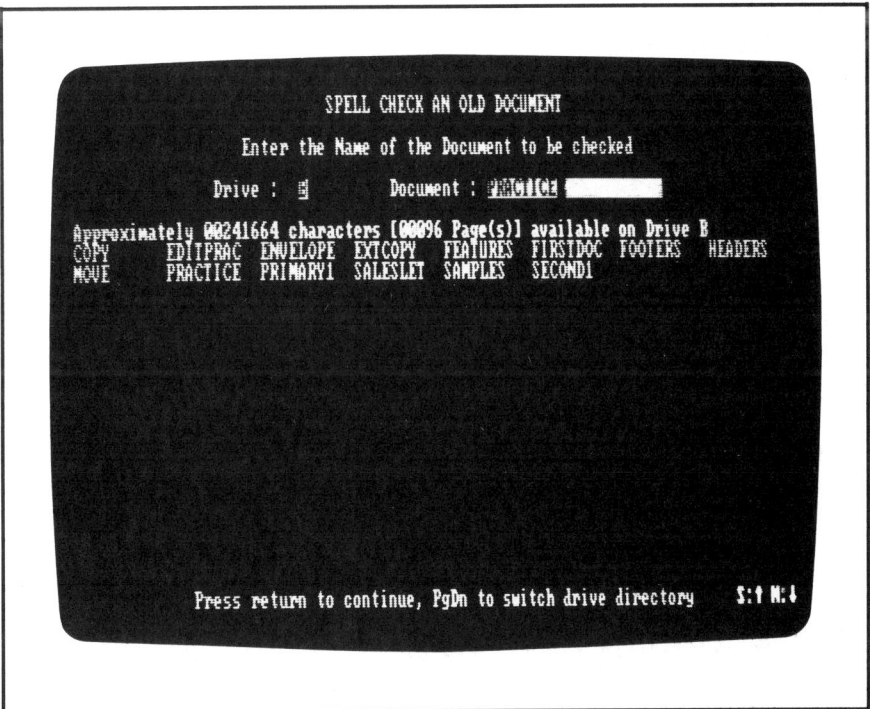

Figure 18.1 – *Spell Check an Old Document screen*

Press F10 and this prompt will display: *OPERATION IN PROGRESS, INSERT DICTIONARY DISK IN DRIVE A—PRESS ANY KEY.* Remove your MultiMate System Disk and insert the dictionary disk in drive A. Press any key to begin the Spell Check process.

At the bottom of the screen, you will see *OPERATION IN PROGRESS* and a running total of *[00000] WORDS MISSPELLED [00000] WORDS TOTAL.* When these numbers stop increasing and are preceded by the prompt, *OPERATION COMPLETE—PRESS ANY KEY TO CONTINUE,* press any key. You will then see the prompt, *RE-INSERT SYSTEM DISK IN DRIVE A—PRESS ESC TO CONTINUE.*

To correct the errors just found, don't put the system disk back in drive A yet. You will need the dictionary disk in drive A to perform Spell Edit, so press Esc to return to the Main Menu.

So far, you have been given a count of the number of misspelled words and the total number of words, and the system has marked the misspelled words in the document.

To view the marked words, press 1 and return to access *Edit an Old Document* from the Main Menu. Follow the screen prompts to get to the first page of the document. Those flashing characters you see mark the words not found on the dictionary disk.

HOW TO SPELL CHECK A PORTION OF A DOCUMENT

You just Spell Checked your entire document, but you can also Spell Check a portion of a document. For example, if you added three new paragraphs to a document you had previously Spell Checked, you wouldn't want to Spell Check the whole thing again. In this case, you would place the cursor on the first character of the new section and press Ctrl-F10 (the Spell Check combination). The prompt *CHECK WHAT?* displays at the upper right of the screen. This is your invitation to highlight everything you want to Spell Check. (See Chapter 4 for highlighting techniques.) After you highlight the section, press Ctrl-F10. Follow the screen prompt and *INSERT DICTIONARY DISK IN DRIVE A—PRESS ANY KEY.*

As when you initiated the procedure from the Main Menu, the screen displays *[00000] WORDS MISSPELLED [00000] WORDS TOTAL* and the first characters of those words in the checked section which weren't found on the dictionary disk are left flashing. You would then be ready to correct the incorrectly spelled words by using one of the following two techniques.

MANUALLY CORRECTING ERRORS
IDENTIFIED BY SPELL CHECK

Once the Spell Check function has marked errors, you can manually correct them. If you don't have many errors to correct and you don't want to add any words to the custom dictionary, use the following manual method.

Press Ctrl-F1 (*GO TO PLACE MARK*) to move the cursor to each marked word. Remove the place mark by typing over the flashing character and then, if it is wrong, correct the word using regular editing procedures such as Insert and Delete.

Press Ctrl-F1 now to move to the first place marked character. If you want to edit the word, do so now; at least replace the flashing character if the word isn't wrong.

USING SPELL EDIT TO CORRECT ERRORS

Spell Edit provides another, more automatic, way to correct errors in your document. *Note:* You can use the Spell Edit function only after you have completed the Spell Check procedure to identify errors.

Begin with the document on the screen and the cursor located at the beginning of the text you want to Spell Edit. *Note:* If you have just completed a Spell Check and are back at the Main Menu, use *Edit an Old Document* to bring the document to the screen.

Press Alt-F10 (the Spell Edit combination) and follow this screen prompt if it appears: INSERT DICTIONARY DISK IN DRIVE A—PRESS ANY KEY. Remove the MultiMate system disk and insert the dictionary disk and press any key. If you left the dictionary disk in drive A after the Spell Check, Spell Edit starts immediately.

The screen will display several lines of the document and the menu in Figure 18.2 The cursor will be under the first place marked character.

Note: If you now were to get the message: UNABLE TO FIND THE NEXT MISSPELLING—PRESS ANY KEY, check to see that none of the following is true:

1. You are trying to Spell Edit a document that hasn't yet been Spell Checked, so has no place markers.

2. Your text had no errors so has no place markers.

3. Before you began Spell Edit, you placed the cursor *after* the last error so in its forward search no place markers were found.

Here are what the menu choices mean.

0 Add this word to the Custom Dictionary

You can choose to add a word to the Custom Dictionary. If the word is correct and one which you think you will use again in a

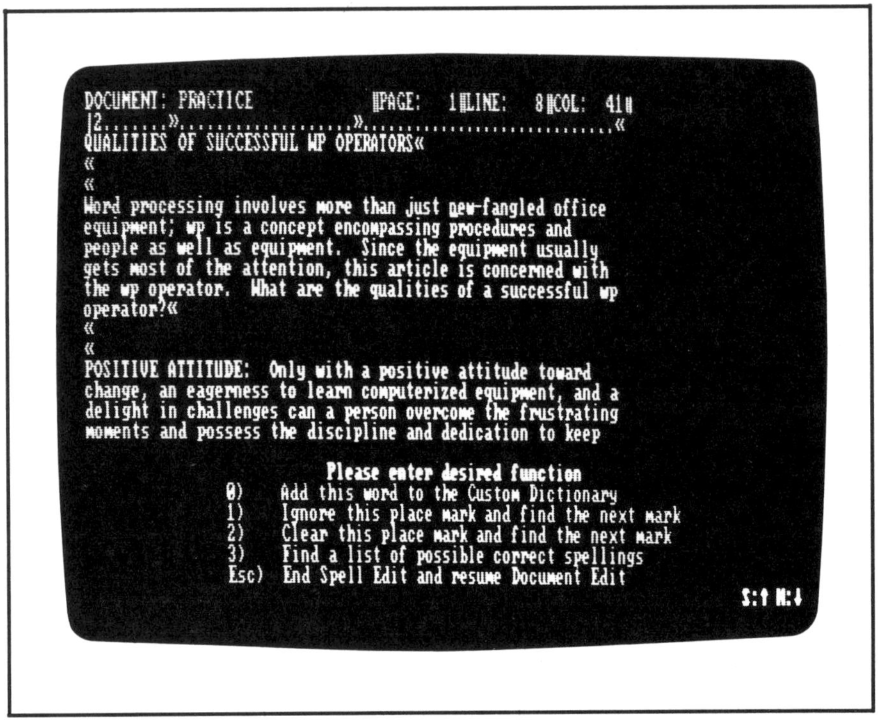

Figure 18.2 – Spell Edit menu

document, press 0. The next time you use the word, it won't be identified as an error. Adding a word to the dictionary disk doesn't automatically erase the place markers on other occurrences of that word throughout the rest of the document.

When you press 0, if the cursor is under a word that begins with a capital letter, this prompt appears: *ADDING TO CUSTOM DICTIONARY: IS CAPITALIZATION REQUIRED?* (the word appears here) *ENTER 'Y' FOR YES, 'N' FOR NO.* If you decide the word should always be capitalized, press Y. The system lets you know it's *ADDING TO CUSTOM DICTIONARY:* (the word appears here).

When you press 0, if the cursor is under a word followed by a period, this prompt appears: *ADDING TO CUSTOM DICTIONARY: IS ENDING PERIOD REQUIRED?* (the word appears here) *ENTER "Y" FOR YES, "N" FOR NO.* If the period should be part of the word, as in "Mrs.," enter Y. If it shouldn't be, enter N. As before, the system lets you know it's *ADDING TO CUSTOM DICTIONARY:* (the word appears here) so you can see exactly what is being added.

After you finish option 0, the prompt *PRESS ANY KEY TO SEARCH FOR THE NEXT MISSPELLING, OR PRESS ESC TO END SPELL EDIT AND RESUME DOCUMENT EDIT.* Press any key to continue the Spell Edit function or press Esc to end Spell Edit and resume regular document editing. The document will remain on the screen and any remaining place markers will still be flashing.

If you finish your document editing and want to resume Spell Editing, place the cursor before the first place marker and press Alt-F10.

1 Ignore this place mark and find the next mark

If you choose this option, the cursor jumps to the next place marker. This option is useful if you had manually place marked a word because you wanted to check the meaning of it later.

2 Clear this place mark and find the next place mark

This choice will stop the character from flashing and move the cursor to the next marked character. You would use this option if the marked word is correct, but you don't want to add it to the Custom Dictionary because you won't use it again or because you have already added it.

3 Find a list of possible correct spellings

The Spell Check function will suggest a list of possible correct spellings. Press 3 to see the prompt *LOOKING FOR CORRECT SPELLING FOR* (the word appears here). After a pause, the system displays up to nine possible correct spellings of the word in question. Each one is numbered, so press the number of the correct spelling (if any) when you see this prompt: *Enter the number of the word to replace the misspelled word* or press Esc to return to Document Edit. The misspelled word is automatically replaced with the correct one, then the cursor moves to the next place marker.

Note: If the word you are replacing is capitalized, underscored, uppercase, or followed by a punctuation mark or a place marker within the word, the replacement word will have the same characteristics.

When you type, if you know that you are going to Spell Edit and yet you want to place mark a word yourself, place mark a character other than the first one. Spell Check marks only the first character of a word.

Also, a marked word which is followed by a period, such as "et al.," generates possible choices from the system such as "etc.."—for some reason, there are abbreviations on the dictionary disk that are followed by two periods. Be careful to watch for periods when you replace a word with one of MultiMate's options. You need only one period at the end of a sentence—even when a declarative sentence ends in an abbreviation.

Note: You might be surprised at some of the strange choices MultiMate gives you. If you don't want to use any of the options, press Esc to return to Document Edit. In a quick flash, the prompt *TO RESUME SPELL EDIT PRESS ALT F10* appears and is rapidly replaced by *RE-INSERT SYSTEM DISK IN DRIVE A—PRESS ESC TO CONTINUE.* If you press Alt-F10 at this time, nothing happens. If you reinsert the system disk in drive A, you simply have to replace it with the dictionary disk as soon as you tap Alt-F10 to continue Spell Editing again, so I recommend you ignore the *RE-INSERT SYSTEM DISK . . .* prompt, and press Esc instead. This removes the prompt, stops the Spell Edit function with the document still on the screen, and puts you in Document Edit mode. Then you can manually correct the word the cursor is on and press Alt-F10 to restart the Spell Edit function from the present cursor location.

If MultiMate doesn't find any possibilities for correct spelling on the dictionary disk, the prompt *NO CORRECT SPELLINGS WERE FOUND, PRESS ANY KEY TO CONTINUE* displays. After you press a key, you are instructed: *TO RESUME SPELL EDIT, PRESS ALT F10* with a prompt that again disappears very rapidly. Before you resume Spell Editing, however, you should correct the error manually. Press Esc to return to Document Edit mode. Correct the word manually, and then press Alt-F10 to resume Spell Editing.

Esc End Spell Edit and resume Document Edit

Choose this option when you want to stop Spell Editing temporarily (say, to insert a word) or permanently (because you are finished). This prompt displays on the screen: *RE-INSERT SYSTEM DISK IN DRIVE A—PRESS ESC TO CONTINUE.*

Now finish spell editing the document, PRACTICE. Use Spell Edit as many times as practical for the types of errors you need to correct. After all the errors are corrected, press F10 to return to the Main Menu.

A FINAL WORD ABOUT SPELL CHECK AND SPELL EDIT

Spell Check and Spell Edit can be very helpful, especially for long documents. However, they can not replace a human proofreader who understands the nuances of the language. A human can recognize not only misspelled words but also words which, even though they are correctly spelled, don't make sense in the given context. A computer program cannot read for context.

SUMMARY OF OPERATIONS COVERED IN THIS CHAPTER

Spell Checking a Document

1. To begin from within a document, press Alt-8.
2. To begin from the Main Menu, press 8 and return.
3. Name the drive location and the document you want to Spell Check and press return.
4. Indicate the page numbers of pages to be checked and press F10.
5. Replace the system disk in drive A with the dictionary disk and press any key.

6. A prompt tells how many errors were found and the total number of words checked.

Spell Checking a Portion of a Document

1. Place the cursor on the first character of the portion you want to spell check.
2. Press Ctrl-F10.
3. *CHECK WHAT* appears as a screen prompt.
4. Highlight everything you want to Spell Check.
5. Press Ctrl-F10 to indicate everything has been highlighted.
6. Replace the system disk in drive A with the dictionary disk; press any key.
7. A prompt tells how many errors were found and the total number of words checked.

Manually Correcting Errors

1. Place the cursor on the first character of the document.
2. Press Ctrl-F1 (Go To Place Mark) to move the cursor to the first place marker.
3. Use regular editing procedures to correct the error.
4. If no editing is necessary, type the flashing character when the cursor is under it to remove the place mark.
5. Use Ctrl-F1 to move the cursor to the next place marker.
6. Edit the word if necessary and continue in the same manner through the document.

Spell Editing a Document

(Note: It must already have been Spell Checked)

1. From the Main Menu, press 1 and return to access the *Edit an Old Document* function.

2. Follow the screen prompts to name the document and get the first page on the screen. (If the document is already on the screen, place the cursor on the first character of the document.)

3. Press Alt-F10 to begin the Spell Edit process.

4. Replace the system disk in drive A with the dictionary disk and press any key.

5. A menu appears under the text and the cursor will be under a flashing character.

6. Choose one of the options on the menu by typing a number; follow the prompts.

7. After you have dealt with the last place marker, the function is over.

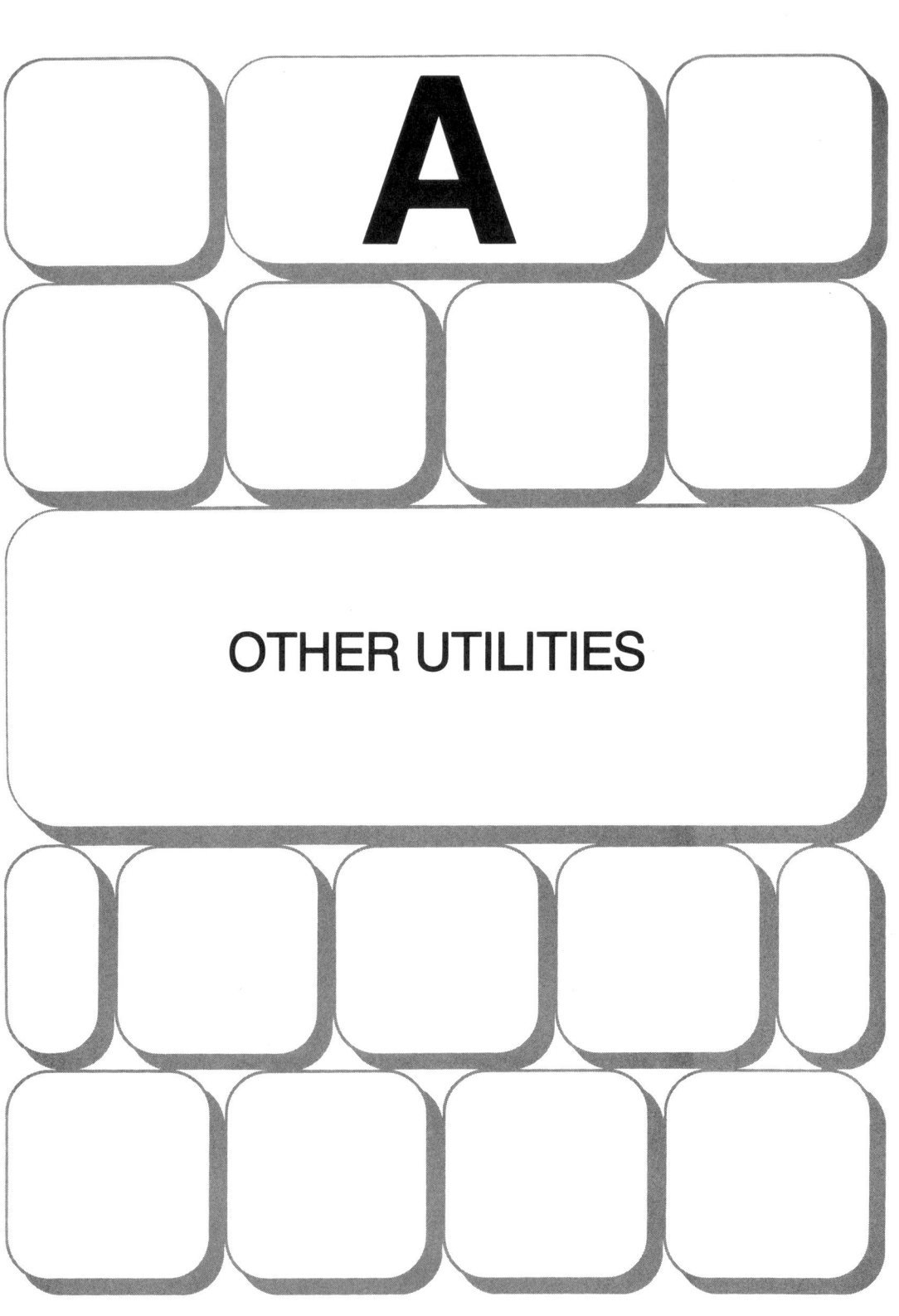

A

OTHER UTILITIES

The Other Utilities Menu

You can change MultiMate defaults by using the Other Utilities Menu. When the Main Menu is on the screen, type 7 and press return. The four choices of the Other Utilities Menu appear on the screen. These are shown in Figure A.1.

Edit System Format Line

If the system or default format line doesn't give you the line length, vertical spacing, and tab settings used for the type of work you will be doing most frequently, the default settings can be changed with the following procedure.

1. From the Other Utilities Menu type 1 and press return to select *Edit System Format Line.*

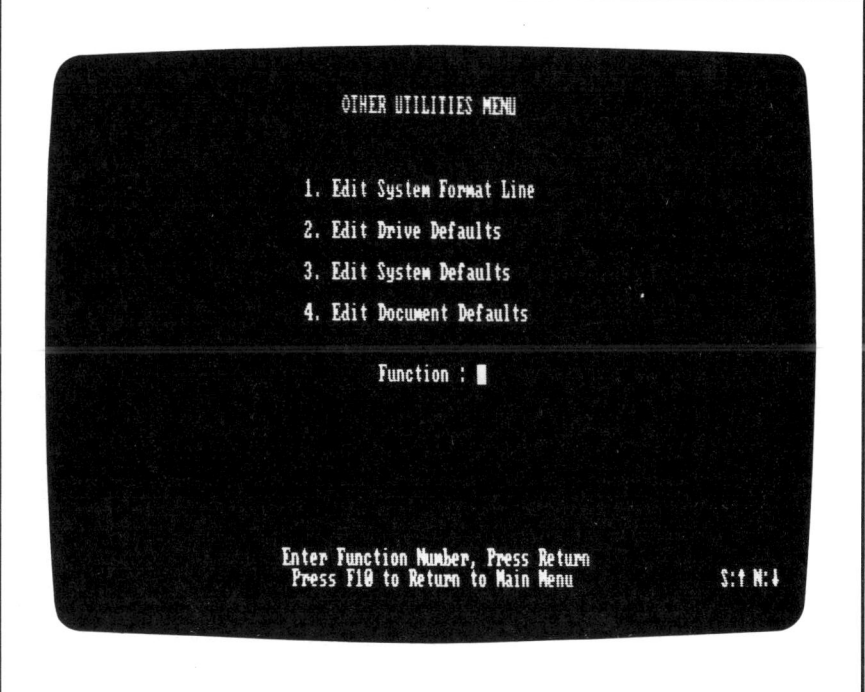

Figure A.1 – Other Utilities Menu

2. Make the changes you want on the System Format Line Modification screen that appears.
3. Press F10 to return to the Main Menu.

Edit Drive Defaults

The Edit Drive Defaults option is used to configure (set up) MultiMate to match your computer system. With the Other Utilities Menu on the screen, type 2 and press return to access the Drive Default Modification screen.

The system is typically configured for two floppy disk drives when the disks are shipped. You will need to change this screen if you have a hard disk drive or more than two floppy drives.

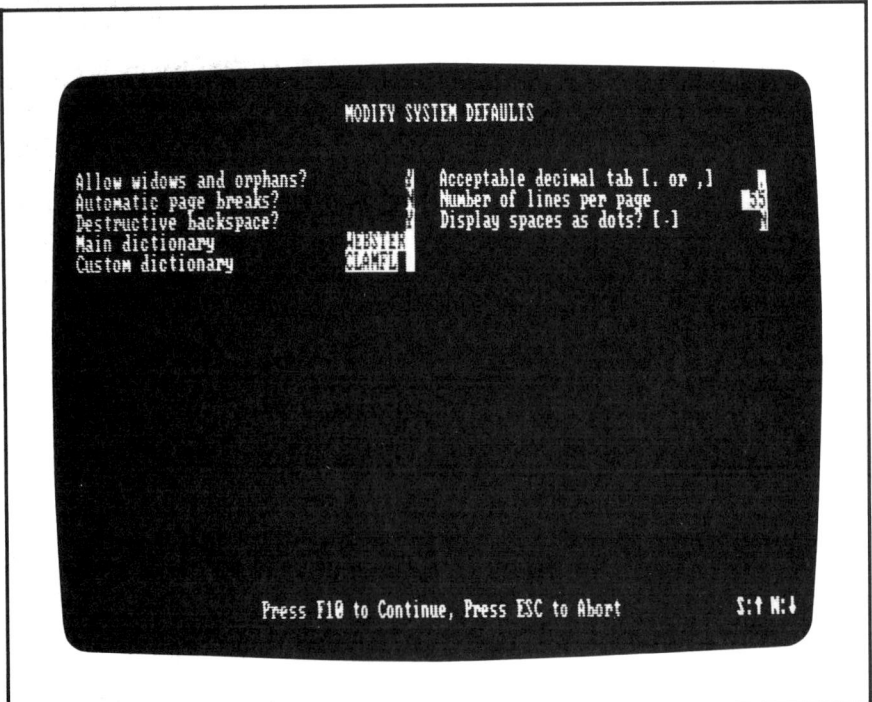

Figure A.2 − Modify System Defaults screen

If you wanted your documents to be stored on the same disk as the MultiMate program, you would change the document drive to A. When you are finished making your changes, press F10 to return to the Main Menu.

Edit System Defaults

To change the Modify Document Defaults screen permanently, pick the third choice on the Other Utilities Menu, *Edit System Defaults,* by typing 3 and pressing return. As illustrated in Figure A.2, the choices on this menu are the same as the ones which appear as you create a new document and which were discussed in Chapter 2.

There are also some additional options. The *Destructive backspace?* category allows you to set the backspace key to be destructive if you wish (see Chapter 1 for discussion of the backspace key).

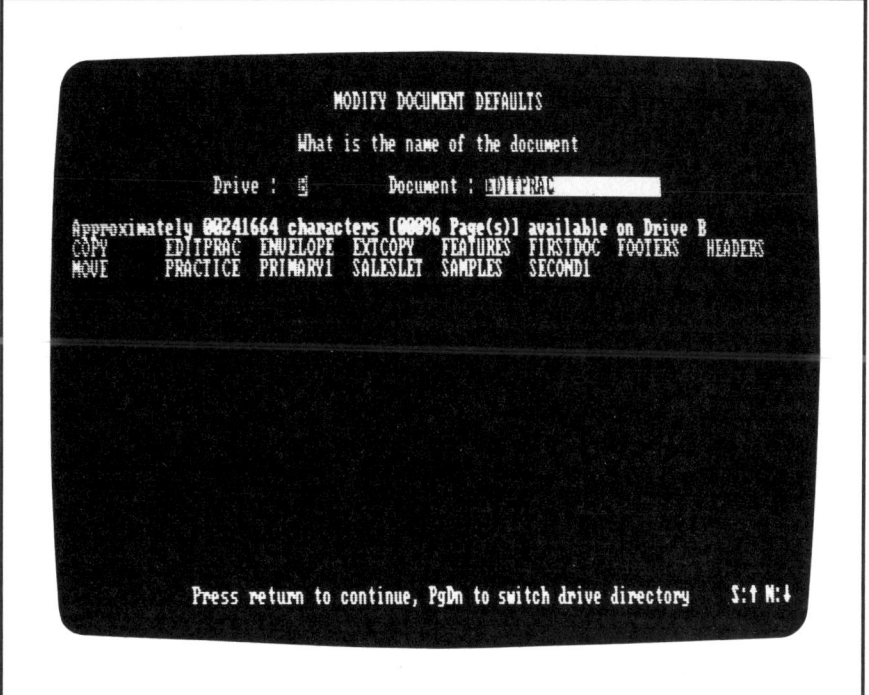

Figure A.3 – Modify Document Defaults: first screen

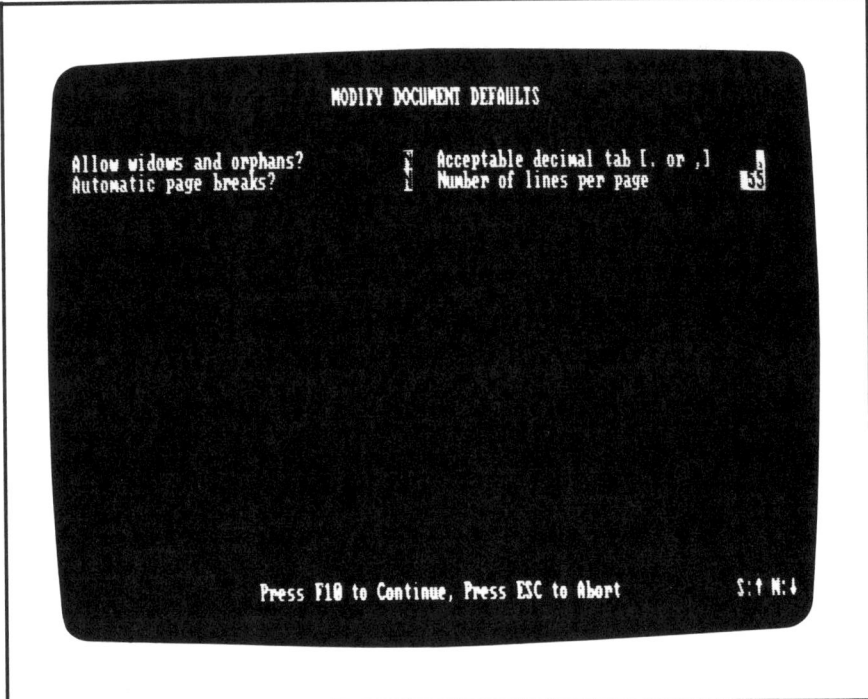

Figure A.4 – *Modify Document Defaults: second screen*

You also can choose to display spaces as dots. If you type Y here, the system will display a dot instead of a blank area for a space. Even if the document was created with blank spaces instead of dots, when you change the *N* to *Y* in answer to this question, dots will display in all documents later called to the screen. The other two *Dictionary* notations refer to the Spell Check and Spell Edit functions, which are covered in Chapter 18.

Note: Changes you make on this screen will be the defaults whenever you create a new document.

Edit Document Defaults

Use *Edit Document Defaults* when you want to change the document defaults *after* a document has been created. From the Other Utilities Menu type *4* and press return to choose *Edit Document*

Defaults and display the Modify Document Defaults screen as shown in Figure A.3.

Then name the document you want changed. Check to be sure that the document is on the drive named, and press return. The screen shown in Figure A.4 then appears.

To make changes, position the cursor with the cursor-moving keys and use strikeover to change the defaults to the ones you want. Press F10 twice to complete the operation and return to the Main Menu. When you next access the document, it will be governed by these new defaults. Of course, *previous* page breaks, widows and orphans, etc., would not be affected, but if you automatically repaginated now, the new default values would be used.

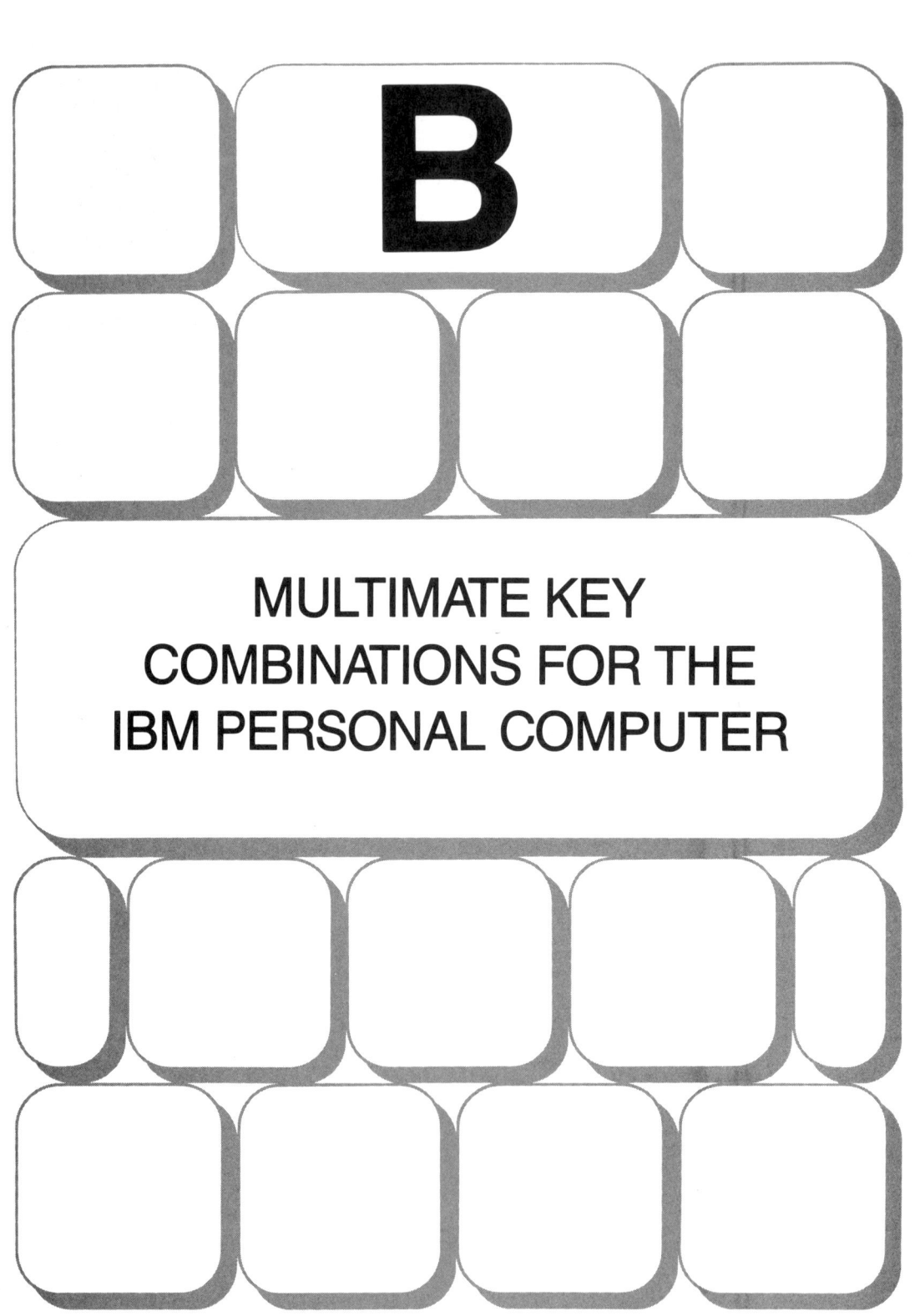

B

MULTIMATE KEY COMBINATIONS FOR THE IBM PERSONAL COMPUTER

MULTIMATE KEY COMBINATIONS FOR THE IBM PERSONAL COMPUTER

Auto Underline—Alphanumeric	Alt- ± (plus/equals key)
Auto Underline—Text	Alt- = (hyphen/underline key)
Back Tab	shift-⇌ (tab key)
Bold Print	Alt-Z
Case Significant (for Search or Replace)	Alt-G
Center	F3
Column Manipulation—Copy	shift-F3 F8
Column Manipulation—Delete	shift-F3 Del
Column Manipulation—Insert	shift-F3 Ins
Column Manipulation—Move	shift-F3 F7
Copy	F8
Create a New Document (From within a Document)	Alt-2
Decimal Tab	shift-F4
Delete	Del
Document Handling Utilities (From within a Document)	Alt-6
Draft Print	Alt-D
Edit Old Document (From within a Document)	Alt-1
End of Page	Ctrl-End
End of Screen	End
Enhanced Print	Alt-N
Escape (quit)	Esc
External Copy	shift-F8

Footer	Alt-F
Format—Change	F9
Format—Current	shift-F9
Format—Delete	Del F9 Del
Format—Page	Alt-F9
Format—System	Ctrl-F9
Go To Page Number	F1 [page number]
Go To Place Mark	Ctrl-F1
Hard Space	Alt-S
Header	Alt-H
Help	shift-F1
Home	Home
Hyphen (Soft)	shift-F7
Indent	F4
Insert	Ins
Key Procedures—Build	Ctrl-F5
Key Procedures—Execute	Ctrl-F8
Key Procedures—Pause	Ctrl-F6
Key Procedures—Prompt	Ctrl-F7
Library Attachment	shift-F5
Library Entry	F5
Line Highlighting	Alt-F6
Merge Code	Alt-M
Merge Print Utility (From within a Document)	Alt-5
Move	F7
Next Page	Ctrl-PgDn
Next Screen	PgDn
Next Word	Ctrl-→ (right cursor mover)
Other Utilities (From within a Document)	Alt-7
Page Break	F2
Page Combine	shift-F2
Page Down	PgDn

Page/Line Length Set	Alt-F2
Page Up	PgUp
Paragraph Highlighting	Alt-F8
Pause Printer—From Printer Controls	Printer On line key or Pause key
Pause Printer—From Document	Alt-P
Previous Page	Ctrl-PgUp
Previous Screen	PgUp
Previous Word	Ctrl-← (left cursor mover)
Print Document (From within a Document)	Alt-3
Print Pitch	Alt-C
Print Screen	shift-PrtSc
Printer Control Utilities (From within a Document)	Alt-4
Repaginate	Ctrl-F2
Replace—Format Line	shift-F6 F9
Replace—Word or Character String	shift-F6
Required Page Break	Alt-B
Return	↵ (return)
Return to DOS (From a Document)	Alt-9
Save	shift-F10
Save/Exit Document	F10
Scroll Cursor Left	Alt-F3
Scroll Cursor Right	Alt-F4
Search—For Format Line	F6 F9
Search—For Word or Character String	F6
Sentence Highlighting	Alt-F7
Set Place Mark	Alt-F1
Shadow Print	Alt-X
Single Character Delete	− (grey minus key)

Single Character Insert	+ (grey plus key)
Spell Check	
(From within a Document)	Alt-8
Spell Edit	Alt-F10
Stop Printer	Ctrl-Break 1
Subscript	Alt-W
Superscript	Alt-Q
Tab	⇆ (tab key)
Top of Page	Ctrl-Home
Underline	shift- — (hyphen/underline key)
Word Highlighting	Alt-F5, or space bar
£(U.K. pound symbol)	Alt-L

INDEX

Acceptable Decimal Tab Default, 20
Advancing Through Document Summary Screen, 18
Alternate Key, 2, 30, 54–55
Alternating Footers, 143
Attach a Library Document, 127–128
Auto Page Numbering
  See Header/Footer
Auto Underline-Alphanumeric, 77
Auto Underline-Text, 76
Automatic Footers, 146–147
Automatic Headers, 144–146
Automatic Page Breaks, 20, 59

Background Printing, 90
Backspace, 5
Backtab/Tab, 3, 30
Bold Print, 95

Caps Lock, 4
Case Blind Search, 118
Case Significant Search, 118
Centering, 69–70
Changing Number of Lines Per Page, 59–60
Characters Defined, 117
Column Copy, 156
Column Delete, 154–155
Column Insert, 153–154
Column Mode, 156
Column Move, 155–156
Combine Pages, 61
Control Key, 2, 29–30
Copy Text, 108–111
Copy a Document, 161, 163
Copy From Another Document, 111–112
Create a Library Document, 125–127
Create a New Document, 15
Create New Pages, 60–61

Creation Date, 170
Current Date Is, 91
Current Time Is, 91
Cursor, 3, 29–33, 63, 64
Crusor-Moving Keys, 5
Custom Dictionary, 184 187–191

Date, 7
Decimal Tabs, 72–73
Default, 16, 85, 86
Default Document Drive, 84
Default Pitch, 88
Dehighlighting, 43–44
Delay Print Until Date Is, 91
Delay Print Until Time Is, 91
Delete a Document, 165–166
Delete Format Line, 55
Delete More Than One Character, 40–41
Delete Page Break, 61
Delete Required Page Break, 63
Delete Single Character, 37–38
Delete Spooler Entry, 90
Delete With Replace, 120
Destructive Backspace, 197
Deunderline, 76
Discretionary Replace, 119–120
Disk Drives, 6, 25
DOS (Disk Operating System), 6–8
Document Handling Utilities, 161
Document Page Length, 89
Document Summary Screen, 17–19
Double Strike, 95
Draft Print, 87, 95
Drive Default Modification Screen, 196–197
Drive Directory, 16

Edit An Old Document, 35, 86

Edit Document Defaults, 198–199
Edit Drive Defaults, 196–107
Edit Printer Defaults, 100
Edit System Defaults, 197–198
Edit System Format LIne, 195–196
Editing, 35–47
End Spell Edit, 191
Enhanced Print Mode, 95–97
Envelopes, 139
Escape, 2
Error Status, 99
Exiting the Document, 24–26
External Copy, 111–112

First Page Bin Number, 89
First Page Number Header/Footer, 88
Footer, 88, 143, 148
Foreground Printing, 90
Format, 49
Format Change, 52–54
Format Line, 21, 50–55
Format Line Replace, 121–122

Generic Printer Action Table 89–90
Global Replace, 119–120

Hard Copy, 83
Hard Hyphen, 74
Hardspaces, 73–74
Header, 88, 143, 148
Help Facility, 10–11
Highlighting, 41–44
Home Position, 32

Identification Key Words, 169
Indent, 70–72
Insert, 39–40, 51–52
Insert More Than One Character, 38–39
Insert Single Character, 36–37

Key Procedure File, 175–179
  Build, 176–177
  Edit, 178–179
  Execute, 175, 177–178
Keys, 1–5
Keystroke, 175

Left Margin, 86
Letter Key, 2
Library, 18, 125
  Attach, 127–128
  Create, 125–127
  Recall, 128–129
Line Spacing, 51
Lines Per Inch, 88
Loading DOS and MultiMate, 6–8

Main Menu, 8, 84
Margins, 49–50
Merge Function, 133–136
Merge Print Utility, 136–138

Modification Date, 170
Modify Document Defaults Screen, 19–20, 135, 199
Modify Printer Defaults, 100
Move, 105–108
Move a Document, 163–165
Move Through Pages, 63–64

Null Footer, 148
Null Header, 148
Num Lock, 4
Number of Lines Per Page, 21
Number of Original Copies, 89
Number/Symbol, 2
Numeric Key Pad, 2

On Hold Status, 99–100
Orphans, 19
Other Utilities Menu, 195

Page Break, 60, 62
Page Combine, 61
Page Down Key, 16, 32–33
Page Numbers on Long Documents, 143–144
Parallel Port, 89
PATs, 89–90
Pause Printer, 93–94
Place Mark, 64
Primary Document, 133–134
Print a Document, 84
Print Document Summary, 90, 168
Print In Background/Foreground, 90
Print Screen, 51
Print Screen Key, 93
Print Spooling Statistics, 90
Printer, 83–84
Printer Control Utilities, 100
Printer Needs Attention, 94
Printer Number, 89
Printer Pitch, 88
Printer Queue Control, 94, 99–100
Printer Type, 89, 100
Printing Merged Documents, 136–139
Prompts, 9

Recall Library Entries, 128–129
Recall Name for Library Entry, 126
Rename a Document, 167–168
Repaginate, 61–62
Replace, 119–120
Resume Spell Edit, 19
Return, 4
Right Justification, 87, 100
Right Margin, 86
Roman Numerals, 149

Saving a Document, 45–46
Screen Capacities, 30–31, 50
Scrolling, 31

Search, 117–119
Search Document Summary Screens, 168–170
Secondary Document, 134–136
Serial Port, 89
Shadow Print, 95
Sheet Feeders, 89–90
Shift Keys, 3
Single Strike, 95
Soft Hyphen, 74
Source/Target, 162
Space Bar, 3
Special Print Modes, 95–97
Spell Check, 183, 184–186
Spell Edit, 183, 187
Spool, 83
Spool Queue, 83
Spooling Statistics, 83

Start Print at Page Number, 86
Status Line, 21
Stop Print at Page Number, 86
Stopping Printing, 94–95
Strikeover, 35–36
Submit a Document to Print, 84–90
Subscript, 77–78
Superscript, 77–78
System Defualt Format Line, 21–22, 51

Tab/Backtab, 3, 30
Target/Source, 162
Time, 7
Toggle Key, 4, 5
Top Margin, 87

Widows, 19
Word Wrap/Wraparound, 22–24, 73
Writing Line, 49–50

Selections from The SYBEX Library

Computer Specific

IBM PC AND COMPATIBLES

OPERATING THE IBM PC NETWORKS
Token Ring and Broadband
by Paul Berry
363 pp., illustr., Ref. 307-4
This tells you how to plan, install, and use either the Token Ring Network or the PC Network. Focusing on the hardware-independent PCN software, this book gives readers who need to plan, set-up, operate, and administrate such networks the head start they need to see their way clearly right from the beginning.

THE ABC'S OF THE IBM PC
by Joan Lasselle and Carol Ramsay
143 pp., illustr., Ref. 102-0
This book will take you through the first crucial steps in learning to use the IBM PC.

THE IBM PC-DOS HANDBOOK
by Richard Allen King
296 pp., Ref. 103-9
Explains the PC disk operating system. Get the most out of your PC by adapting its capabilities to your specific needs.

BUSINESS GRAPHICS FOR THE IBM PC
by Nelson Ford
259 pp., illustr. Ref. 124-1
Ready-to-run programs for creating line graphs, multiple bar graphs, pie charts and more. An ideal way to use your PC's business capabilities!

THE IBM PC CONNECTION
by James Coffron
264 pp., illustr., Ref. 127-6
Teaches elementary interfacing and BASIC programming of the IBM PC for connection to external devices and household appliances.

DATA FILE PROGRAMMING ON YOUR IBM PC
by Alan Simpson
219 pp., illustr., Ref. 146-2
This book provides instructions and examples for managing data files in BASIC Programming. Design and development are extensively discussed.

THE MS-DOS HANDBOOK
by Richard Allen King (2nd Ed)
320 pp., illustr., Ref. 185-3
The differences between the various versions and manufacturer's implementations of MS-DOS are covered in a clear straightforward manner. Tables, maps, and numerous examples make this the most complete book on MS-DOS available.

ESSENTIAL PC-DOS
by Myril and Susan Shaw
300 pp., illustr., Ref. 176-4
Whether you work with the IBM PC, XT, PC jr. or the portable PC, this book will be invaluable both for learning PC DOS and for later reference.

Software Specific

SPREADSHEETS

MASTERING SUPERCALC 3
by Greg Harvey
300 pp., illustr., Ref. 312-0
Featuring Version 2.1, this title offers full

coverage of all the sophisticated features of this third generation spreadsheet, including spreadsheet, graphics, database and advanced techniques.

DOING BUSINESS WITH MULTIPLAN
**by Richard Allen King
and Stanley R. Trost**
250 pp., illustr., Ref. 148-9

This book will show you how using Multiplan can be nearly as easy as learning to use a pocket calculator. It presents a collection of templates for business applications.

MULTIPLAN ON THE COMMODORE 64
by Richard Allen King
250 pp., illustr. Ref. 231-0

This clear, straightforward guide will give you a firm grasp on Multiplan's function, as well as provide a collection of useful template programs.

WORD PROCESSING

PRACTICAL WORDSTAR USES
by Julie Anne Arca
303 pp., illustr. Ref. 107-1

Pick your most time-consuming office tasks and this book will show you how to streamline them with WordStar.

THE THINKTANK BOOK
by Jonathan Kamin
200 pp., illustr., Ref. 224-8

Learn how the ThinkTank program can help you organize your thoughts, plans and activities.

PRACTICAL MULTIMATE USES
by Chris Gilbert
275 pp., illustr., Ref. 276-0

Includes an overview followed by practical business techniques, this covers documentation, formatting, tables, and Key Procedures.

MASTERING WORDSTAR ON THE IBM PC
by Arthur Naiman
200 pp., illustr., Ref. 250-7

The classic Introduction to WordStar is now specially presented for the IBM PC, complete with margin-flagged keys and other valuable quick-reference tools.

MASTERING MS WORD
by Mathew Holtz
365 pp., illustr., Ref. 285-X

This clearly-written guide to MS WORD begins by teaching fundamentals quickly and then putting them to use right away. Covers material useful to new and experienced word processors.

PRACTICAL TECHNIQUES IN MS WORD
by Alan R. Neibauer
300 pp., illustr., Ref. 316-3

This book expands into the full power of MS WORD, stressing techniques and procedures to streamline document preparation, including specialized uses such as financial documents and even graphics.

INTRODUCTION TO WORDSTAR 2000
**by David Kolodney
and Thomas Blackadar**
292 pp., illustr., Ref. 270-1

This book covers all the essential features of WordStar 2000 for both beginners and former WordStar users.

PRACTICAL TECHNIQUES IN WORDSTAR 2000
by John Donovan
250 pp., illustr., Ref. 272-8

Featuring WordStar 2000 Release 2, this book presents task-oriented tutorials that get to the heart of practical business solutions.

MASTERING THINKTANK ON THE 512K MACINTOSH
by Jonathan Kamin
264 pp., illustr., Ref. 305-8

Idea-processing at your fingertips: from basic to advanced applications, including answers to the technical question most frequently asked by users.

DATABASE MANAGEMENT SYSTEMS

UNDERSTANDING dBASE III PLUS
by Alan Simpson
415 pp., illustr., Ref. 349-X
Emphasizing the new PLUS features, this extensive volume gives the database terminology, program management, techniques, and applications. There are hints on file-handling, debugging, avoiding syntax errors.

UNDERSTANDING dBASE III
by Alan Simpson
250 pp., illustr., Ref. 267-1
The basics and more, for beginners and intermediate users of dBASEIII. This presents mailing label systems, bookkeeping and data management at your fingertips.

ADVANCED TECHNIQUES IN dBASE III
by Alan Simpson
505 pp., illustr., Ref. 282-5
Intermediate to experienced users are given the best database design techniques, the primary focus being the development of user-friendly, customized programs.

MASTERING dBASE III: A STRUCTURED APPROACH
by Carl Townsend
338 pp., illustr., Ref. 301-5
Emphasized throughout is the highly successful structured design technique for constructing reliable and flexible applications, from getting started to advanced techniques. A general ledger program is used as the primary illustration for the examples.

UNDERSTANDING dBASE II
by Alan Simpson
260 pp., illustr., Ref. 147-0
Learn programming techniques for mailing label systems, bookkeeping, and data management, as well as ways to interface dBASE II with other software systems.

ADVANCED TECHNIQUES IN dBASE II
by Alan Simpson
395 pp., illustr. Ref., 228-0
Learn to use dBASE II for accounts receivable, recording business income and expenses, keeping personal records and mailing lists, and much more.

INTEGRATED SOFTWARE

MASTERING 1-2-3
by Carolyn Jorgensen
420 pp., illustr., Ref. 337-6
This book goes way beyond using 1-2-3, adding powerful business examples and tutorials to thorough explanations of the program's complex features. Detailing multiple functions, powerful commands, graphics and database capabilities, macros, and add-on product support from Report Writer, Spotlight, and The Cambridge Spread-sheet Analyst. Includes Release 2.

SIMPSON'S 1-2-3 MACRO LIBRARY
by Alan Simpson
300 pp., illustr., Ref. 314-7
This book provides many programming techniques, macro examples, and entire menu-driven systems that demonstrate the full potential of macros. The full power of 1-2-3 version 2 is laid out in powerful, time-saving business solutions developed by bestselling author Alan Simpson.

ADVANCED BUSINESS MODELS WITH 1-2-3
by Stanley R. Trost
250 pp., illustr., Ref. 159-4
If you are a business professional using the 1-2-3 software package, you will find the spreadsheet and graphics models provided in this book easy to use "as is" in everyday business situations.

THE ABC'S OF 1-2-3 (New Ed)
by Chris Gilbert and Laurie Williams
225 pp., illustr., Ref. 168-3

For those new to the LOTUS 1-2-3 program, this book offers step-by-step instructions in mastering its spreadsheet, data base, and graphing capabilities. Features Version 2.

MASTERING SYMPHONY
by Douglas Cobb (2nd Ed)
763 pp., illustr., Ref. 224-8

This bestselling book has been heralded as the Symphony bible, and provides all the information you will need to put Symphony to work for you right away. Packed with practical models for the business user. Includes Version 1.1.

ANDERSEN'S SYMPHONY TIPS & TRICKS
by Dick Andersen and Janet McBeen
325 pp., illustr. Ref. 342-2

Organized as a reference tool, this book gives shortcuts for using Symphony commands and functions, with troubleshooting advice.

BETTER SYMPHONY SPREADSHEETS
by Carl Townsend
287 pp., illustr., Ref. 339-2

For Symphony users who want to gain real expertise in the use of the spreadsheet features, this has hundreds of tips and techniques. There are also instructions on how to implement some of the special features of Excel on Symphony.

MASTERING FRAMEWORK
by Doug Hergert
450 pp., illustr. Ref. 248-5

This tutorial guides the beginning user through all the functions and features of this integrated software package, geared to the business environment.

ADVANCED TECHNIQUES IN FRAMEWORK
by Alan Simpson
250 pp., illustr. Ref. 257-4

In order to begin customizing your own models with Framework, you'll need a thorough knowledge of Fred programming language, and this book provides this information in a complete, well-organized form.

MASTERING THE IBM ASSISTANT SERIES
by Jeff Lea and Ted Leonsis
249 pp., illustr., Ref. 284-1

Each section of this book takes the reader through the features, screens, and capabilities of each module of the series. Special emphasis is placed on how the programs work together.

DATA SHARING WITH 1-2-3 AND SYMPHONY: INCLUDING MAINFRAME LINKS
by Dick Andersen
262 pp., illustr., Ref. 283-3

This book focuses on an area of increasing importance to business users: exchanging data between Lotus software and other micro and mainframe software. Special emphasis is given to dBASE II and III.

MASTERING PARADOX
by Alan Simpson
350 pp., illustr., Ref. 334-1

Everyone's introduction to this unique, menu-driven dbms, from essential operations to complex uses including PAL programming techniques. There are valuable real-world illustrations including a complete mailing lists system, and an inventory, sales, and purchasing system with automatic multiple-table updating.

JAZZ ON THE MACINTOSH
by Joseph Caggiano and Michael McCarthy
431 pp., illustr., Ref. 265-5

Each chapter features as an example a business report which is built on throughout the book in the first section of each chapter. Chapters then go on to detail each application and special effects in depth.

MASTERING EXCEL
by Carl Townsend
454 pp., illustr., Ref. 306-6

This hands-on tutorial covers all basic

operations of Excel plus in-depth coverage of special features, including extensive coverage of macros.

APPLEWORKS: TIPS & TECHNIQUES
by Robert Ericson
373 pp., illustr., Ref. 303-1
Designed to improve AppleWorks skills, this is a great book that gives utility information illustrated with every-day management examples.

MASTERING APPLEWORKS
by Elna Tymes
201 pp., illustr., Ref. 240-X
This bestseller presents business solutions which are used to introduce Apple-Works and then develop mastery of the program. Includes examples of balance sheet, income statement, inventory control system, cash-flow projection, and accounts receivable summary.

PRACTICAL APPLEWORKS USES
by David K. Simerly
313 pp., illustr., Ref. 274-4
This book covers a breadth of home and business uses, including combined-function applications, complicated tasks, and even a large section on interfacing AppleWorks with the outside world.

Languages

PASCAL

INTRODUCTION TO TURBO PASCAL
by Douglas S. Stivison
268 pp., illustr., Ref. 269-8
This bestseller introduces Pascal programming in the environment of Turbo Pascal, giving realistic examples from the author's programming experience. The focus is on how to get all the benefits offered by this Pascal implementation.

INTRODUCTION TO PASCAL, INCLUDING TURBO PASCAL
by Rodnay Zaks
464 pp., illustr., Ref. 319-8
This new version of the Sybex classic book describes Pascal clearly and quickly. There is a complete set of exercises and answers in both Turbo Pascal and ISO Standard Pascal.

TURBO PASCAL LIBRARY
by Douglas S. Stivison
221 pp., illustr., Ref. 330-9
This presents a collection of proven programs and procedures that express Turbo's style and power. The library includes general-purpose procedures applicable to a wide range of programming projects including games, system utilities, and calculating routines for business and engineering applications. Ideal for students, new programmers, and experienced programmers looking to increase their Turbo resources.

INTRODUCTION TO PASCAL (Including UCSD Pascal)
by Rodnay Zaks
420 pp., 130 illustr., Ref. 066-0
A step-by-step introduction for anyone who wants to learn the Pascal language, describing UCSD and Standard Pascals. No technical background is assumed.

THE PASCAL HANDBOOK
by Jacques Tiberghien
486 pp., 270 illustr., Ref. 053-9
A dictionary of the Pascal language, defining every reserved word, operator, procedure, and function found in all major versions of Pascal.

PASCAL PROGRAMS FOR SCIENTISTS AND ENGINEERS
by Alan R. Miller
374 pp., 120 illustr., Ref. 058-X
A comprehensive collection of frequently used algorithms for scientific and technical applications, programmed in Pascal. Includes programs for curve-fitting, integrals, stastical techniques, and more.

FIFTY PASCAL PROGRAMS
by Bruce H. Hunter
338 pp., illustr., Ref. 110-1
More than just a collection of useful programs! Structured programming techniques are emphasized and concepts such as data type creation and array manipulation are clearly illustrated.

THE C LANGUAGE

UNDERSTANDING C
by Bruce H. Hunter
320 pp., Ref. 123-3
Explains how to program in powerful C language for a variety of applications. Some programming experience assumed.

MASTERING C
by Craig Bolon
400 pp., illustr., Ref. 326-0
Designed for the programming professional, this gives a complete description of C language programming, focusing on how to get the most power, efficiency, and portability out of C.

DATA HANDLING UTILITIES IN C
by Robert Radcliffe and Thomas Raab
500 pp., illustr., Ref. 304-X
This is a "Software Toolkit" of useful C functions, techniques and usable code for commercial application programmers and software developers. Because commercial programs require high user-interaction and permanent files, the book concentrates on data entry, validation, display, and efficient data storage. There is a comprehensive section all about logical data types and another giving sample applications.

Technical

ASSEMBLY LANGUAGE

ASSEMBLY LANGUAGE TECHNIQUES FOR THE IBM PC
by Alan Miller
350 pp., illustr., Ref. 309-0
Any IBM PC user and programmer that wants to learn techniques to get more power from the PC will find the tutorial and program library elements in this title extremely valuable. Programs included in the book allow the reader to do such tasks as transferring WordStar to ASCII and back, switch from color screens to monochrome screens and back, set the printer to any typeface, and more. Techniques are given for the programmer to generate more programs.

PROGRAMMING THE 65816
by William Labiak
350 pp., illustr., Ref. 324-4
Giving the latest in this hot new area of development, this book teaches assembly language programming for the 65816, 65C816, 65S816, and 65SC816 chips. The 65802 is also presented. Step-by-step exercises and tutorials enable the reader to write complete applications programs.

PROGRAMMING THE APPLE II IN ASSEMBLY LANGUAGE
by Rodnay Zaks
519 pp., illustr., Ref. 290-6
All elements of the art of assembly language programming for the current Apple IIc and Apple IIe are covered in Zaks' classic style.

PROGRAMMING THE MACINTOSH IN ASSEMBLY LANGUAGE
by Steve Williams
400 pp., illustr., Ref. 263-9
This is an up-to-date tutorial and reference guide to programming the 68000 in the Macintosh environment. Covering architecture, instruction set, Toolbox, and advanced programming concepts, this is ideal for intermediate to professional applications programmers.

HARDWARE

THE RS-232 SOLUTION
by Joe Campbell
194 pp., illustr., Ref. 140-3
Finally, a book that will show you how to correctly interface your computer to any RS-232-C peripheral.

are different.

Here is why . . .

At SYBEX, each book is designed with you in mind. Every manuscript is carefully selected and supervised by our editors, who are themselves computer experts. We publish the best authors, whose technical expertise is matched by an ability to write clearly and to communicate effectively. Programs are thoroughly tested for accuracy by our technical staff. Our computerized production department goes to great lengths to make sure that each book is well-designed.

In the pursuit of timeliness, SYBEX has achieved many publishing firsts. SYBEX was among the first to integrate personal computers used by authors and staff into the publishing process. SYBEX was the first to publish books on the CP/M operating system, microprocessor interfacing techniques, word processing, and many more topics.

Expertise in computers and dedication to the highest quality product have made SYBEX a world leader in computer book publishing. Translated into fourteen languages, SYBEX books have helped millions of people around the world to get the most from their computers. We hope we have helped you, too.

For a complete catalog of our publications:

SYBEX, Inc. 2021 Challenger Drive, #100, Alameda, CA 94501
Tel: (415) 523-8233/(800) 227-2346   Telex: 336311